GIULIANO HAZAN'S

Thirty Minute
PASTA

100 Quick and Easy Recipes

Photographs by

JOSEPH DE LEO

STEWART, TABORI & CHANG | NEW YORK

For Michela, my little pasta queen

Published in 2009 by Stewart, Tabori & Chang
An imprint of Harry N. Abrams, Inc.

Text copyright © 2009 by Giuliano Hazan
Photographs copyright © 2009 by Joseph De Leo

Library of Congress Cataloging-in-Publication Data:
Hazan, Giuliano.
Giuliano Hazan's Thirty Minute Pasta.
    p. cm.
Includes bibliographical references and index.
ISBN 978-1-58479-807-1 (alk. paper)
1. Cookery (Pasta) 2. Quick and easy cookery.
3. Cookery, Italian. I. Title.
TX809.M17H32 2009
644'.755–dc22   2008053114

Editor: Luisa Weiss
Designer: Susi Oberhelman
Production Manager: Tina Cameron

The text of this book was composed in Andrade and Futura

Printed and bound in China

10 9 8 7 6 5 4 3 2 1

HNA
harry n. abrams, inc.
a subsidiary of La Martinière Groupe

115 West 18th Street
New York, NY 10011
www.hnabooks.com

CONTENTS

SEAFOOD PASTAS

Meat Pastas

INTRODUCTION

In our increasingly busy lives, there seems to be less and less time to cook—yet more and more people are realizing the importance of eating at home, both as a way to strengthen family bonds and as a healthier, more economical alternative to eating out. This creates a yearning to have quality meals prepared at home. The Mediterranean diet of low-fat carbohydrates such as pasta and lots of fresh vegetables and fruits, along with an active lifestyle, has been proven to promote a long and healthy life. Fads may come and go, but the appeal of pasta has endured even the Atkins diet craze. Taking the time to prepare a home-cooked meal may seem like a luxury, but in fact it doesn't need to take longer than going out or even getting take-out. Many of the pasta sauces I prepare at home do not take much longer than boiling the water and cooking the pasta.

There are several myths surrounding the origins of pasta, the best known being that Marco Polo brought it back from China. There is the dubious assertion in Greek mythology that the god Vulcan invented a device that made strings of dough like spaghetti, but in fact Vulcan was a Roman god, not Greek. My favorite is a legend told by the Neapolitan storyteller Matilde Serao in her 1881 short-story compilation, *Leggende Napoletane* (*Neapolitan Legends*). According to this story, in 1220 there lived in Naples a magician by the name of Chico. He rarely came out of his top-floor apartment except for occasional trips to the market to buy various herbs and tomatoes. (Getting tomatoes was a pretty neat trick for Chico to pull off—everybody else in Europe had to wait another 400 years, until well after the discovery of America. But he was a magician, after all.) He spent his days in front of a large bubbly cauldron and his nights poring over ancient texts and manuscripts. After many years of trials and tribulations, he finally succeeded in creating something he knew would greatly contribute to the happiness of mankind.

During all this time, Jovanella, the devious and opportunistic wife of one of the king's kitchen help, had been spying on his every move from her terrace, which gave her a view into Chico's apartment. One day she finally discovered Chico's secret. Jovanella ran to her husband and told him their troubles would be over and they would be rich if he did what she told him. "What must I do?" he asked her. "Go tell the king's chef that I have discovered a new food so exquisite that it deserves to be tasted by His Majesty." Jovanella's husband spoke to the chef, who spoke to the butler, who spoke to a count, who, after much deliberation, spoke to the king. The king, who was getting rather bored with the food he had been eating, eagerly welcomed the opportunity to try something different. So Jovanella was admitted to the royal kitchens and proceeded to prepare what she had seen the magician create. She combined flour, water, and eggs to form a dough that she then painstakingly pressed out until it was as thin as parchment. She cut it into strips that she left out to dry. She then cooked onions, meat, and tomatoes over very low heat for a long time until they formed a sauce. When it was time to eat, she cooked the pasta in boiling water, drained it, and tossed it with the sauce and "the famous cheese from Parma." The king was so impressed by what Jovenella had made that he asked her how she had managed to come up with such a remarkable invention. She answered that an angel had revealed it to her in a dream. The king ordered that she be rewarded handsomely for having made such an important contribution to the happiness of mankind. Soon every noble in the area offered Jovanella rich rewards so their cooks could learn how to make her incredible recipe. One day Chico was walking down the street and smelled the aroma of his wonderful invention coming from one of the houses. Incredulous, he walked in and asked what was being prepared. He was told of a wonderful new food that an angel had revealed to a woman in her sleep.

It was such a blow to him that he ran home, packed all his things, and disappeared—no one heard from him again.

The fact is that pasta has been around for a very long time, and not just in Italy. The discovery of a well-preserved sealed earthenware bowl of millet noodles in an archeological site in northwestern China indicates that the Chinese were already eating noodles 4,000 years ago. In fact, it's likely that since humans began cultivating wheat 10,000 years ago, they have been making some kind of dough with it, whether it was cooked on hot stones or boiled. There is a reference to what could be pasta cooked by boiling in the Talmud, where it refers to "itrium" as a kind of boiled dough that was used in Palestine between the third and fifth centuries A.D. It is pretty much undisputed now that pasta existed in Italy before Marco Polo returned from China in 1295, and it's likely that it was introduced in Italy by the Arab invaders of Sicily. The word *maccaruni* means "to make dough by force" in Sicilian dialect. A small-scale industrial production of dried pasta in Trabia, a village outside of Palermo, is mentioned in an Arab geographer's 1154 book, *A Diversion for the Man Longing to Travel to Far-Off Places*. The first documented recipe for pasta seems to be in *De arte Coquinaria per vermicelli e maccaroni siciliani* (*The art of cooking Sicilian vermicelli and macaroni*), written in the eleventh century by Martino Corno, chef to the matriarch of Aquileia.

Italians, of course, love pasta. In 2004, the Italian newspaper *Il Corriere della Sera* reported that according to a survey commissioned by the Italian National Research Council, one-third of Italians would rather dig into a dish of pasta than have sex. Half of those interviewed said they could not imagine living without pasta. The mere thought of taking pasta away from an Italian's diet would be cause for severe depression. I know I experience withdrawal symptoms if I go more than a few days without it. During some of the most intense periods of recipe testing for this book, we were eating four or five pasta dishes *a day*. Yet if even a few days went by without pasta, my family would inevitably begin asking for a good dish of it. In most parts of Italy, pasta is as commonplace as bread and is eaten daily—not, however, as a whole meal. It is usually served as a first course, in smaller portions than what people are accustomed to in the United States, followed by a smaller meat or fish course. Most of my readers will probably serve the dishes in this book as a meal, perhaps with a salad, and the serving size indicated reflects that. To serve it as a first course, in the traditional Italian style, increase the number of servings to six.

There are many variations of pasta throughout Italy, including pasta made with buckwheat flour, chickpea flour, chestnut flour, or farro, an ancient Etruscan grain similar to spelt that has recently been growing in popularity. The two kinds of pasta you are most likely to encounter, however, are flour-and-water pasta and egg pasta. The latter is often referred to as "homemade pasta" and is best when made by hand. To make shaped egg pasta, the dough is rolled out until it is very thin and then cut into noodles of various widths. It is a delicate pasta that becomes porous and quite absorbent when it is rolled out and stretched, making it best suited to butter-based sauces, sauces with cream, and sweeter, milder sauces in general. Flour-and-water pastas, on the other hand, are made with durum wheat, a harder flour than is used with egg pasta, so the resulting dough is much firmer and better suited to factory production. To make shapes, the dough is pushed, or extruded, through dies. This creates sturdier pasta with a texture best suited to olive oil–based sauces and more robustly flavored sauces such as those with capers, anchovies, olives, or hot red

pepper. Homemade egg pasta is not necessarily better than store-bought flour-and-water pasta; it is simply different. The favorite Roman midnight snack of *aglio e olio*, an olive oil and garlic sauce with the optional addition of parsley and hot red pepper, is ideally suited to firm-textured spaghetti or spaghettini, but would not taste good with homemade fettuccine (or any homemade egg pasta).

Though the theme of this book is quick sauces you can make in about thirty minutes, I did not want to limit myself to sauces for flour-and-water pastas, because there are so many sauces for egg pasta that are very quick and simple to make. Ideally I would encourage you to use homemade whenever egg pasta is called for. You can make large batches and dry it so that you'll always have some on hand. Once dried, egg pasta will easily keep for several months. Otherwise, use a premium brand of the dried egg noodles you will find in the dry goods section. Don't use the "fresh" pastas that are sold in refrigerated cases. Refrigeration has a detrimental effect on pasta. Moisture causes pasta to spoil, which is why keeping pasta fresh requires preservatives; drying it will preserve it naturally. Using a premium brand of flour-and-water pasta is also very important. If you taste a simple sauce with an industrially mass-produced brand side by side with a premium artisanal brand, you'll be amazed at the difference in flavor and texture. Artisanally made pastas are extruded through bronze dies rather than Teflon, giving them a wonderful texture that sauces can cling to. Of course, the quality of the wheat makes a huge difference in the flavor. Artisanal pasta makers are very particular about blends and varieties of wheat—sometimes even single varietal heirloom wheat is used.

Recipes sometimes make cooking—which should be a spontaneous, fluid activity—into a static and somewhat disjointed one. One of the principal culprits is the need to stop and measure, something I never do unless I am testing or creating a recipe. If I need chopped onions, I'll decide whether I should use half (or a quarter) of a small, medium, or large onion, not how many tablespoons. If I need garlic, it's either one or two small or large cloves. So rather than specifying a third of a cup of chopped onion—and causing you to cut into another if you don't have enough, or throwing some away if you have too much—I call for halves of onions and numbers of garlic cloves instead. When it comes to herbs, it occurred to me that it would be useful to know if the five sprigs of parsley you have left in the refrigerator will yield the tablespoon of parsley a recipe calls for. So in the ingredient list I put the number of sprigs of an herb you'll need, and in the recipe I specify the amount you should use in teaspoons and tablespoons. This is so you don't end up putting in twice the amount of oregano I intended—but again, small variations in the amounts are okay. I also guide you as to when ingredients need to be chopped or sliced, because prepping everything before you begin cooking can waste quite a bit of time, and I realized I never cook that way.

Cooking for someone is one of the most loving gifts you can bestow, because you are giving a little of yourself. Occasional dinner parties and special occasions need not be the only time to cook for someone. After all, aren't you and your family as deserving of your love as dinner party guests? What I hope to do with this book, in addition to sharing one of my favorite foods with you, is to make it easier for you to give yourself and your family the gift of home cooking whenever you are in the mood for pasta.

GIULIANO HAZAN
Sarasota, Florida

The Many Shapes of Pasta

PASTA CAN BE FOUND IN AN EXTRAORDINARY NUMBER of varieties and shapes. A comprehensive list would be encyclopedic in length, not to mention that a definitive lexicon is not really possible. The same shape of pasta can have a different name depending on the region it is from. Sometimes the same name can even be used for a number of different shapes, depending on where you are. When I first visited Verona to create a cooking school in its beautiful wine country, I was quite taken aback when I ordered lasagne at a restaurant and was served what to me were tagliatelle, noodles that are slightly wider than fettuccine (which, by the way, are called *lasagnette* in Verona). The dish of baked lasagne that the rest of Italy is familiar with is called *pasticcio* in Verona. Filled pasta shapes can be even more confusing. The square-shaped filled pasta known as *tortelloni* in the Romagna part of Emilia Romagna may be called *ravioli*, *tortelli*, or *pansotti* in other regions. In Bologna, which is in the Emilia part of Emilia Romagna, *tortelloni* are the large version of *tortellini*, the bishop's hat–shaped pasta, which in Romagna are instead called *cappelletti*.

The variety of pasta shapes that are available is not simply fanciful: most sauces are best suited to certain shapes. Long pasta shapes, such as spaghetti and linguine, are usually best with smoother sauces that don't have chunks of vegetables or meat. Chunky sauces are best suited to tubular shapes such as penne, rigatoni, and maccheroni, and many of the special shapes such as fusilli, shells, and cartwheels. Listed below are the shapes that you are most likely to encounter in Italy and that I use in this book. I have divided them into two main categories: flour-and-water pastas and egg pastas.

Flour-and-water pasta shapes:

SPAGHETTI: Probably the best known of all pasta shapes, spaghetti are a masterful invention. Their sturdy texture makes them a perfect vehicle for a wide variety of sauces, but not usually meat sauces or ones with large chunks. **IDEAL PAIRINGS:** Spaghetti Carbonara, page 131; Spaghetti with Cheese and Pepper, page 70; Spaghetti with a Savory Tomato Sauce, page 121.

SPAGHETTINI: Literally, little or thin spaghetti. It's especially important to use a premium brand of spaghettini and not to overcook them. They go well with simple, savory sauces, but not heavy sauces. **IDEAL PAIRINGS:** Spaghettini with Tomatoes and Olives, page 67; Spaghettini with Olive Oil and Garlic, page 49; Spaghettini with Fresh Herbs, page 48.

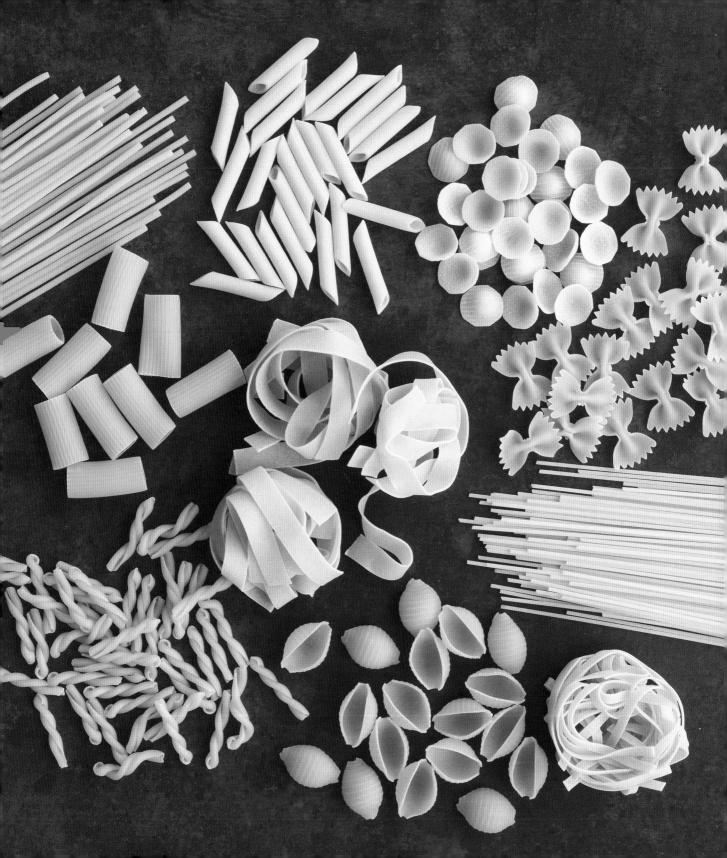

LINGUINE: Linguine means "little tongues" and in Italy they are used mostly in the southern part of the country. They go well with sturdier pasta when a bit more surface area for sauce is desired. **IDEAL PAIRINGS:** Linguine with a Pink Shrimp Sauce, page 100; Linguine with Lobster and Asparagus, page 110; Linguine with Fresh Tomato, Basil, and Mozzarella, page 93.

BUCATINI: Also called *perciatelli* by some manufacturers, these hollow spaghetti are wonderful with the robust sauces found in south-central Italy. **IDEAL PAIRINGS:** Bucatini with Fresh Tomatoes and Thyme, page 158; Bucatini with a Spicy Tomato Sauce, page 146.

FUSILLI: This fun shape can be either long, resembling a coiled telephone cord, or short like a corkscrew. They are great with sauces with chunky bits that cling well to the pasta. **IDEAL PAIRINGS:** Fusilli with Yellow Squash and Grape Tomatoes, page 83; Fusilli with Green and Yellow Peppers, page 74; Fusilli with Sausage, Ricotta, and Fresh Tomatoes, page 165.

PENNE: Penne are probably the most commonly used of the tubular pastas. They are available either smooth or ridged and in a variety of sizes. Penne go well with tomato sauces, sauces that have small chunks, and some heavier cheese sauces. **IDEAL PAIRINGS:** Penne with Four Cheeses, page 87; Penne with Mushrooms and Ham, page 159; Penne with Tomatoes and Prosciutto, page 152.

MACCHERONI: Historically the name was synonymous with *pasta* when it first made its appearance in the aristocratic courts of southern Italy. Now *maccheroni* refers to a straight-edged tubular pasta, which like penne can be either smooth or ridged. Many sauces that are good with penne are also good with maccheroni. **IDEAL PAIRINGS:** Maccheroni with Pancetta and Ricotta, page 134; Maccheroni with Tomatoes and Sage, page 148.

RIGATONI: These large, wonderfully chewy and satisfying tubes are a classic, popular shape in Italy. They are traditionally served with meat sauces, but are also good with chunky vegetable sauces. **IDEAL PAIRINGS:** Rigatoni with a Veal Roast Sauce, page 157; Rigatoni with Onions, Pancetta, and Pecorino, page 139.

CAVATAPPI: Their name means "corkscrews," but unlike the short fusilli, they are hollow inside, somewhat like an enlarged section of the long fusilli. Their twisted shape wraps itself around chunky vegetable sauces wonderfully, and they are also great in certain hearty soups. **IDEAL PAIRINGS:** Vegetable Soup with Pasta, page 29; Egg Drop Soup with Zucchini, Amalfi Style, page 34.

ORECCHIETTE: These are a specialty of Apulia, where they are usually served with a broccoli rabe sauce; the name means "little ears." They are traditionally made by hand from a flour-and-water pasta dough pressed between the thumb and palm. **IDEAL PAIRING:** Orecchiette with Broccoli, page 124.

FARFALLE: *Farfalle* in Italian means "bowties." Their convoluted shape makes them excellent for meat sauces and chunky vegetable sauces. **IDEAL PAIRINGS:** Farfalle with Fresh Salmon, page 118; Farfalle with Peas and Lettuce, page 137; Farfalle with Salami and Tomatoes, page 153.

CONCHIGLIE: The name means "shells," and conchiglie are available in a variety of different sizes. The smallest ones are usually used in soups, the larger ones for sauces. One of my favorite pairings is with butter and cheese because there is so much surface area for the sauce to coat. **IDEAL PAIRINGS:** Shells with Sausage and Cream, page 160; Shells with Butter and Cheese, page 95.

RUOTE: Also called *ruote di carro*, which means "cartwheels," this pasta shape pairs well with chunky vegetable sauces, meat sauces, and sauces that are good with rigatoni.

LUMACHE: *Lumache* is Italian for "snails," and they are similar to the curled shape of a snail's shell. Meat sauces go especially well with this pasta. An ideal pairing is Shells with Sausage and Cream, page 160.

STROZZAPRETI: The name, which literally means "priest stranglers," supposedly came about after a priest's gluttony led to a fatal encounter with this pasta. They are, of course, quite harmless and are traditionally made by hand from flour-and-water pasta dough in the south or from egg pasta in Romagna. They are about 1½ inches long and resemble a piece of stretched telephone cord. They are similar to gemelli, or "twins," and casarecci, and would go well with sauces I've paired with fusilli in this book.

Egg Pasta Shapes

FETTUCCINE: This is probably the best known of the ribbon pastas. It is narrower than tagliatelle and best suited to delicate cream-based sauces. Its most famous pairing is probably the Roman Alfredo sauce. **IDEAL PAIRINGS:** Fettuccine Alfredo, page 44; Fettuccine with Spring Vegetables, page 46; Fettuccine with Lemon, page 45.

TAGLIATELLE: Bologna is the home of tagliatelle, flat noodles slightly wider than fettuccine. In 1972 the Accademia della Cucina Italiana, an organization devoted to preserving authentic Italian cuisine, created a replica of the "ideal" tagliatella in gold. Its width was determined to be exactly 1/12.270 the height of the Torre Asinelli, Bologna's famous medieval tower, or about 6.5 millimeters. Its most classic match is with Bolognese meat sauce. **IDEAL PAIRINGS:** Tagliatelle with a Quick and Simple Meat Sauce, page 156; Tagliatelle with Prosciutto, page 130; Tagliatelle with Peas, page 53.

PAPPARDELLE: These are wide ribbons that in Bologna are also known as *larghissime*, which means "very wide." They are good with most sauces for tagliatelle and where you want lots of surface area to be coated with the sauce. **IDEAL PAIRING:** Pappardelle with Shiitake Mushrooms, page 143.

CAPELLI D'ANGELO: The name means "angel hair" because capelli d'angelo are extremely thin. They are traditionally served in a soup of homemade meat broth. In Italy they are never served with sauce because they are too light and delicate.

TAGLIOLINI: Except for capelli d'angelo, this is the narrowest of the ribbon pastas. It is occasionally used with a sauce but more commonly served in homemade broth. **IDEAL PAIRINGS:** Tagliolini in Broth, page 38; Tagliolini with White Truffle, page 43.

MALTAGLIATI: The name literally means "badly cut," and they are cut from a rolled-up sheet of pasta into irregular triangles. To approximate them you can break up pappardelle into 1-inch pieces. **IDEAL PAIRINGS:** Pea Soup with Pasta, page 33; Cannellini Bean and Pasta Soup, page 28.

SOUP PASTA: There are many different types of small shapes that are used in soups, some of which probably exist simply to appeal to children, such as alphabet pasta, stars, tiny rings, and shells. Some are small tubes and some resemble rice or melon seeds. They are best suited to simple broths and light soups. An ideal pairing is in the Children's Pasta Soup, page 39.

The PASTA PANTRY

Cooking simply and with few ingredients requires great care and high-quality ingredients. There are many pasta dishes that can be prepared with a well-stocked pantry and refrigerator, without having to go shopping first. Non-perishables such as dried porcini, capers, and anchovies are all very useful things to have on hand. What perishables to keep on hand will depend on how often one cooks. Here I list the items I always have a supply of in my kitchen.

PANTRY NON-PERISHABLES

OLIVE OIL: The Romans considered olive oil the noble condiment and butter fit only for barbarians. Among the things Romans brought with them when they settled in conquered lands were olive trees. Never use anything other than extra-virgin olive oil. The degree of "virginity" of an olive oil is determined by the level of acidity. The lower the acidity, the better the oil. To be labeled extra-virgin, its acidity cannot be more than 0.8 percent by law. Most good extra-virgin oils are less than 0.5 percent. In addition, the oil must be obtained from the first pressing of the olives without the use of heat or any chemicals, hence the term "cold press" so often seen on labels. When I use olive oil it is for the flavor it gives a dish, so I always try to use the best. It is just as important to use a high-quality olive oil for cooking as it is for dressing salads and drizzling on a finished dish. If you were to taste a dish of spaghetti with olive oil and garlic made with a premium olive oil next to one made with an inexpensive olive oil, you would be amazed at the difference.

SALT: Salt is essential in coaxing flavor out of food. Using spices instead of salt only succeeds in adding extraneous flavors that may mask ingredients instead of enhancing their taste. I rarely give measurements for salt because seasoning with salt is something you really need to develop a feeling for. I use sea salt exclusively because it doesn't add any bitterness or aftertaste.

BOUILLON CUBE: When I do not have any homemade meat broth available, I prefer using a good bouillon cube rather than canned broth. To approximate the lighter flavor of Italian broth, use 1 large cube to 4–5 cups water.

HOT RED PEPPER FLAKES: Italian food is not generally spicy, but occasionally we do like a little heat. In Italy I like using whole dried hot peppers, but in the States I usually use hot red pepper flakes, which are easier to find. If you can get the whole dried peppers, use one whole dried pepper in place of $\frac{1}{8}$ teaspoon flakes.

BEANS: I am a firm believer in good-quality canned beans. Fresh beans, when available, are certainly superior, but otherwise I highly recommend the convenience of canned beans. The varieties used in this book are cannellini beans, chickpeas, and cranberry beans (*borlotti* in Italian).

DRIED PORCINI: Though not really a substitute for fresh porcini, the luscious Italian wild mushrooms, dried porcini deliver a concentrated burst of wild mushroom flavor. They can be used to add porcini flavor to regular cultivated mushrooms. Look for packages with slices of the caps as well as the stems. They will keep a long time—several months.

CAPERS: Capers are available preserved either in salt or in vinegar. The advantage of the ones preserved in vinegar is that they last a long time, even after the jar is opened. Unfortunately, capers in vinegar inevitably take on a vinegar flavor that will not go away even if you rinse them. Capers preserved in salt do not last as long, but the salt imparts no flavor, so they only taste of capers. You can tell when they spoil because the salt turns yellow. When using salted capers, first soak them in several changes of water to rinse away the salt. Once the container is opened, both kinds must be refrigerated.

ANCHOVIES: Look for anchovies packed in glass jars, which are usually of better quality than anchovies packed in tins and much easier to store in the refrigerator once opened. Anchovies, contrary to what you might think, do not add a fishy flavor to a sauce. Most of the time you can't even tell they are there. However, they do add a distinctive richness of flavor to many pasta sauces.

BREADCRUMBS: The breadcrumbs used in the recipes in this book are plain, fine, dry breadcrumbs, not seasoned crumbs. If you'd like to make your own, remove the crust from day-old bread and bake in the oven at 250°F for about 5 minutes. When the bread has cooled, pulse it in a food processor until you get fairly even-sized crumbs that are not too fine. Use for recipes that call for coarser crumbs. For recipes that call for fine crumbs, pulse them finer, then put the breadcrumbs through a medium-mesh strainer. Store in a jar in the pantry. They'll keep for several weeks.

PANTRY PERISHABLES

GARLIC: An Italian pantry without garlic is inconceivable; however, less garlic is used in Italian cooking than most people believe. Garlic's rich and slightly pungent flavor should complement a dish, not dominate it. When you buy garlic, make sure it is firm, with no green shoots sprouting. Store garlic in a dry, ventilated location, not a refrigerator, for no more than a couple of weeks.

ONIONS: I use sweet yellow onions predominantly, but unless sweet onions are specifically called for, regular yellow onions are fine. They should be stored just like garlic, unless you have a cut piece of onion left over, which should be wrapped in plastic wrap and placed in the refrigerator.

FRESH TOMATOES: Whenever tomatoes are called for in this book, I always mean fresh tomatoes. Canned tomatoes are better suited to recipes where they cook for 45 minutes or longer, which breaks down their acidity, resulting in a concentrated tomato flavor. The recipes in this book use tomatoes for their fresh flavor and are cooked briefly. Out of season, when I am limited to supermarket tomatoes, I like using what are called "ugly ripe" tomatoes. Otherwise, choose the best-looking ripe tomato you can find. Don't keep tomatoes in the refrigerator, as it will rob them of flavor.

In the Refrigerator

PARMIGIANO-REGGIANO: The king of cheeses and the cheese of kings—well, fortunately not anymore. Parmigiano-Reggiano is a cow's-milk cheese of incomparable flavor, texture, and richness, prized as a table cheese as well as a grating cheese. Made the same way for eight centuries, this cheese is still dependent on the skill of it's maker, passed on from generation to generation. Only buy cheese that has the words *Parmigiano-Reggiano* imprinted on the rind. Always grate Parmigiano-Reggiano as close to when you need it as possible. Never buy pre-grated cheese. Even if you are certain it is the real thing, by the time you use it, it will have dried and lost much of its fragrance. A choice piece will easily keep for several months. When you get home, divide it into two or three pieces so that you only unwrap and re-wrap one smaller piece at a time. The other pieces will keep better without being opened all the time. Keep the pieces in individual Ziploc bags, making sure to squeeze all the air out. It's possible that some mold may form on the surface. It's nothing to be concerned about—simply scrape it off with a knife.

PECORINO ROMANO: Often referred to as simply *Romano*, Pecorino Romano is an aged sheep's-milk cheese that is intensely flavored and a bit sharper than Parmigiano-Reggiano. It is better suited to boldly flavored olive oil–based sauces such as the spicy Amatriciana on page 146 or the roasted pepper sauce on page 78.

BUTTER: I use unsalted butter exclusively. First of all, I prefer the flavor. Second, salt is used primarily as a preservative so the butter will keep longer; consequently, unsalted is likely to be fresher. That said, even unsalted butter keeps well for several weeks, so I always have a "backup pound" on hand.

FRESH HERBS: If you have the inclination, growing your own herbs is the easiest way to always have some on hand. Basil, mint, rosemary, sage, thyme, marjoram, and oregano are all fairly easy to grow, even indoors on a windowsill. If it is not practical to grow your own herbs, buy them as you need them. Most supermarkets now have a pretty good selection year-round. Keep herbs in the refrigerator in a Ziploc bag. Wrapping them in damp paper towels keeps the leaves too wet and causes them to rot faster. I always strip the leaves from the stems and chop the leaves just before adding them to what I'm cooking. Chopping herbs ahead of time causes them to turn brown and lose their fragrance.

PARSLEY: Parsley is one herb I have found impractical to grow. Mostly it's because I use it faster than it grows; it is the most commonly used fresh herb in Italian cuisine. In Italy there is a saying that if you run into someone all the time they are "like parsley." The only parsley I use is flat-leaf Italian parsley. Curly parsley is rather harsh and not as fragrant. After washing parsley, make sure to pat the leaves dry with paper towels before chopping, or it clumps together. The best way to keep parsley in the refrigerator is with the stems immersed in a glass of water, like a bouquet of flowers. It will keep for a week or more if it is very fresh.

OLIVES: I find pitted olives in brine tend to lose their flavor because the hole in the center, where the flesh is not protected by skin, soaks up the watery brine. Since I always slice olives anyway, it does not take any more time or work to slice the flesh from the pit. Only buy olives as needed because they do not keep long outside their brine, even in the refrigerator.

PANCETTA: Pancetta is basically Italian bacon. The main difference is that pancetta is not smoked but is air-cured, just like prosciutto, and can be eaten as is. If it is well wrapped, it will keep for a week in the refrigerator.

How *to* Cook Pasta

For perfectly cooked pasta, follow these simple rules:

1. Use plenty of water—about 6 quarts for 1 pound of pasta. Without enough water, the pasta will not cook evenly and may stick together.

2. Add about 2 tablespoons salt (for 6 quarts water) after the water boils and before putting the pasta in. Remember, the amount of salt you are putting in depends on how much water you have. The more water, the more salt is needed. Without salt the pasta will have no flavor. If you salt the water before it boils, it will take longer to come to a boil.

3. Put the pasta in and cook uncovered until done. Italians like their pasta al dente, meaning firm when you bite it. How firm depends on where you are in Italy. The farther south you travel, the firmer the pasta becomes. It should not be crunchy in the middle, however. Cooking time varies by shape and manufacturer. Some brands offer fairly reliable cooking instructions on the packaging, some do not. Tasting is the only surefire method of determining if it's done and something my children love to assist with.

4. Stir the pasta occasionally while it's cooking, especially in the first few minutes, when the starch is at its stickiest. As long as you have plenty of water, keep it at a rolling boil, and stir periodically, there is no need to add oil to prevent the pasta from sticking.

5. When the pasta is done, drain it but never rinse it. Rinsing will make the pasta cold and washes away the coating of starch that allows sauces to cling to it. Instead, toss it with the sauce right away so that it will immediately absorb the flavor and not stick together.

Pasta
SOUPS

Cannellini Bean *and* Pasta Soup

Minestra di Cannellini e Pasta

Minus the pasta, this soup spans at least three generations. My mother learned it from her father. Then it became one of my father's favorites. He is particularly fond of beans, and this is a thick soup of all beans and very little else. The little else though, is garlic and parsley, which give cannellini beans an immensely satisfying flavor. I've added pasta to make the soup substantial enough for a meal.

SERVES 4

1 large clove garlic

3 tablespoons extra-virgin olive oil

3 cups (2 15-ounce cans) canned cannellini beans, drained

Salt

Freshly ground black pepper

3–4 springs flat-leaf Italian parsley

1 large beef bouillon cube

4 ounces dried egg noodles, such as tagliatelle or pappardelle

1. Peel the garlic and finely chop it. Put it with the olive oil in a 4- to 6-quart soup pot and place over medium-high heat. After the garlic begins to sizzle, add the cannellini beans and season with salt and pepper. Cook, stirring occasionally, for about 5 minutes.

2. While the beans are cooking, finely chop enough parsley to measure 1 tablespoon.

3. After the beans have cooked for 5 minutes, add 2 cups water and the bouillon cube and cover the pot. Once the soup has come to a boil, break the egg noodles into approximately 1-inch pieces and add them to the soup. Lower the heat to medium, add the parsley, and cook, covered, until the pasta is al dente. Serve hot.

Vegetable Soup *with* Pasta

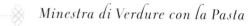

Minestra di Verdure con la Pasta

Often Italian vegetable soups require long cooking times to achieve the desired depth of flavor. This soup, however, cooks fairly quickly, so the vegetables retain a fresh and fragrant flavor. I like a larger, more substantial pasta shape here, particularly the tubular, corkscrew-shaped cavatappi.

SERVES 4

1. Peel the onion and finely chop it. Peel the carrot and cut it into small dice, about ⅛ inch. Put the butter in a 3- to 4-quart soup pot and place over medium-high heat. When the butter begins to melt, add the onion and carrot and sauté until the onion turns a rich golden color, about 5 minutes.

2. While the onion is sautéing, cut the prosciutto into ⅛-inch dice. Cut off the root end of the leeks and trim the tough dark-green tops of the leaves. Cut the leeks into ½-inch chunks, put them in a bowl, and cover with water. Swish the leeks with your hands to loosen any dirt.

3. When the onion is ready, add the prosciutto and sauté briefly until it loses its raw color, about 1 minute. Lift the leeks out of the water in the bowl and add them to the pot. Season lightly with salt and continue cooking, stirring periodically.

4. Wash the zucchini, remove the ends, and cut into ½-inch chunks. Peel the tomatoes and coarsely chop. Add the zucchini and tomatoes to the pot. Season with pepper and lightly with salt. Add 4 cups water and the bouillon cube, raise the heat, and when the soup comes to a boil, lower the heat to medium. Cook, covered, for 15 minutes, then add the pasta and frozen peas. Cook until the pasta is al dente. Stir in the grated Parmigiano-Reggiano and serve hot.

½ small yellow onion

1 medium carrot

2 tablespoons butter

1 ounce prosciutto, sliced ⅛ inch thick

2 medium leeks

Salt

1 zucchini (6–7 ounces)

¾ pound tomatoes

Freshly ground black pepper

1 large beef bouillon cube

6 ounces cavatappi

4 ounces frozen peas

¼ cup freshly grated Parmigiano-Reggiano

Bean *and* Pasta Soup

Pasta e Fagioli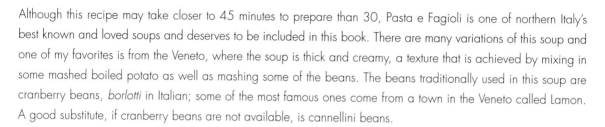

Although this recipe may take closer to 45 minutes to prepare than 30, Pasta e Fagioli is one of northern Italy's best known and loved soups and deserves to be included in this book. There are many variations of this soup and one of my favorites is from the Veneto, where the soup is thick and creamy, a texture that is achieved by mixing in some mashed boiled potato as well as mashing some of the beans. The beans traditionally used in this soup are cranberry beans, *borlotti* in Italian; some of the most famous ones come from a town in the Veneto called Lamon. A good substitute, if cranberry beans are not available, is cannellini beans.

SERVES 4

1 medium boiling potato

½ small yellow onion

1 medium carrot

1 medium celery stalk

2 medium cloves garlic

4 tablespoons extra-virgin olive oil

3 cups (2 15-ounce cans) canned cranberry or cannellini beans, drained

Salt

Freshly ground black pepper

8 ounces fresh tomatoes

1 large beef bouillon cube

1 bay leaf

5 ounces short tubular pasta

3–4 sprigs flat-leaf Italian parsley

¼ cup freshly grated Parmigiano-Reggiano

1. Wash the potato, put it in a pot, and cover it with water. Place over high heat and bring to a boil. Lower the heat to medium and cook until the potato is tender, about 30 minutes.

2. While the potato is cooking, peel and finely chop the onion. Peel the carrot and the back of the celery stalk and cut both into small dice. Peel and lightly crush the garlic. Peel the tomatoes and coarsely chop them. When the potato is done, put the onion, carrot, celery, and garlic in a 4- to 5-quart soup pot together with 3 tablespoons of olive oil. Place over medium-high heat and sauté until the vegetables begin to brown, about 5 minutes.

3. While the vegetables are sautéing, peel the boiled potato.

4. When the vegetables are ready, remove and discard the garlic cloves. Add the chopped tomatoes and continue cooking for 5 minutes. Add 2 cups of the canned beans, season with salt and pepper, and cook, stirring, for about a minute. Add 5 cups water and the bouillon cube. Mash the potato with a food mill or potato ricer and add to the pot. Do the same with the remaining cup of canned beans. Add the bay leaf, cover the pot, and raise the heat to high. When the soup comes to a boil, lower the heat to medium and cook for 15 minutes.

5. Add the pasta and cook, covered, until the pasta is al dente, stirring often. Chop enough parsley to measure 1 tablespoon. When the pasta is done, stir in the chopped parsley and serve. Drizzle some of the remaining olive oil and sprinkle freshly grated Parmigiano-Reggiano over each serving.

PEA SOUP *with* PASTA

 Pasta e Bisi

Risi e Bisi is a classic rice and pea soup that is traditionally prepared in June when the exquisitely sweet peas of Peseggia, north of Venice, are in season. Sometimes it is so thick it is eaten with a fork instead of a spoon. It occurred to me that I could replace the rice with pasta, and thus was born Pasta e Bisi, admittedly my own invention. If fresh peas are in season, it is definitely worth the time to shell them, but I've also tried it with frozen peas, with good results.

SERVES 4

1. Peel the onion and finely chop it. Put the butter in a 4- to 6-quart soup pot, add the chopped onion, and place over medium-high heat. Sauté until the onion turns a rich golden color, about 5 minutes.

2. While the onion is sautéing, shell the peas, if using fresh.

3. When the onion is ready, add the peas and season with salt and pepper. If using fresh, sauté for about a minute, then add 4 cups of water and the bouillon cube. When the broth comes to a boil, lower the heat to medium and cook, covered, for 20 minutes. If using frozen peas, sauté them for about 5 minutes, then add the water and bouillon cube and cook, covered, for 10 minutes after the broth comes to a boil.

4. While the soup is simmering, finely chop enough parsley to measure 1½ tablespoons. Break the egg noodles into approximately 1-inch pieces and add them to the soup together with the parsley. Cook, covered, until the pasta is al dente and serve at once.

½ medium yellow onion

3 tablespoons butter

1¾ pound fresh peas
(or 12 ounces frozen peas)

Salt

Freshly ground black pepper

1 large beef bouillon cube

5–6 sprigs flat-leaf Italian parsley

4 ounces dried egg noodles, such as tagliatelle or pappardelle

Egg Drop Soup *with* Zucchini, Amalfi Style

Zuppa Amalfitana alle Zucchine

This pasta soup is adapted from a recipe my mother learned from Pierino Iovene, who many years ago owned an amazing seafood restaurant, Il Gambero Rosso, in my mother's hometown of Cesenatico. A native of Amalfi and a very gifted cook, Pierino would periodically prepare some of his native specialties for us, one of which was a delicious zucchini egg drop soup. I've replaced the potatoes he used with a corkscrew-shaped, tubular pasta and discovered his soup is also delicious as a pasta soup. Don't use smaller soup pasta shapes, as they are not substantial enough here.

SERVES 4

½ small yellow onion

3 tablespoons extra-virgin olive oil

1 ounce pancetta, sliced ⅛ inch thick

¾ pound zucchini

Salt

Freshly ground black pepper

½ pound tomatoes

6 ounces cavatappi

6–8 fresh basil leaves

1 egg

1. Peel the onion and finely chop it. Put it with the olive oil in a 4- to 6-quart soup pot and place over medium-high heat. Sauté until the onion turns a rich golden color, about 5 minutes.

2. While the onion is sautéing, cut the pancetta into small ⅛-inch dice. Wash the zucchini, remove the ends, and cut it into chunks no larger than ½ inch.

3. When the onion is ready, add the pancetta and sauté until it loses its raw color, about 1 minute. Add the zucchini and season with salt and pepper. Sauté the zucchini until it just begins to brown, 3 to 4 minutes.

4. While the zucchini is sautéing, peel the tomatoes and coarsely chop them. When the zucchini is ready, add the tomatoes. Season lightly with salt, cook for about 3 more minutes, then add 5 cups water. Cover the pot and, once the soup comes to a boil, reduce the heat to medium. Cook until the zucchini is quite tender, 10 to 12 minutes.

5. When the zucchini is tender, add the pasta. Coarsely shred the basil and add it to the soup. Cook until the pasta is al dente.

6. While the pasta is cooking, crack the egg in a small mixing bowl and whisk it until the yolk and white form a homogeneous mixture. As soon as the soup is ready, remove it from the heat and pour the egg into the soup in a thin, steady stream while stirring constantly. Serve at once.

Neapolitan Maccheroni Soup

 Zuppa Napoletana coi Maccheroni in Brodo Colorito

Brodo colorito means "colored broth" and refers to the reddish hue the tomato paste gives this soup. The flavor is simple, direct, and satisfying. The broth is neither a homemade meat broth nor made from bouillon cubes; it is created from the combination of flavors in the soup. The shape I like best here is a short tubular soup pasta, smaller than what one usually thinks of as maccheroni, though at one time in Naples, *maccheroni* was simply a generic term for pasta.

SERVES 4

1. Peel the onion and finely chop it. Put the olive oil in a 3- to 4-quart soup pot, add the chopped onion, and place over medium-high heat. Sauté until the onion turns a rich golden color, about 5 minutes.

2. While the onion is sautéing, finely dice the pancetta. When the onions are ready, add the pancetta and ground beef. Season with salt and pepper and cook until the meat just begins to brown, 1 to 2 minutes. Add the nutmeg and stir in the tomato paste. Add 4 cups water, cover, and raise the heat to high. When the soup comes to a boil, lower the heat to medium and cook for 20 minutes.

3. Add the pasta and cook until it is al dente. Mix in the grated Parmigiano-Reggiano and serve hot.

1 medium yellow onion

3 tablespoons extra-virgin olive oil

2 ounces pancetta, sliced ⅛ inch thick

8 ounces ground beef chuck

Salt

Freshly ground black pepper

¼ teaspoon freshly grated nutmeg

2 tablespoons tomato paste

6 ounces short tubular pasta for soup

½ cup freshly grated Parmigiano-Reggiano

Broccoli Soup *with* Pasta

Zuppa di Pasta e Broccoli

My family loves broccoli sautéed with garlic and olive oil, so I decided to try it in a soup with pasta. Broccoli's rich and nutty flavor makes a great broth for this soup and the pasta absorbs some of that flavor, making the soup more substantial. It is also very quick and easy to prepare.

SERVES 4

2 medium cloves garlic

Salt

¾ pound broccoli florets

2 tablespoons extra-virgin olive oil

Freshly ground black pepper

1 large beef bouillon cube

6 ounces short tubular pasta, or other dried small pasta shape for soup, such as ditalini or small shells

1. Fill a pot with water that will accommodate the broccoli and place over high heat.
2. Peel and finely chop the garlic.
3. When the water is boiling, add 1 teaspoon salt and put in the broccoli. Cook until tender, about 5 minutes after the water comes back to a boil. Drain the broccoli and set aside.
4. Put the garlic and olive oil in a 4- to 6-quart soup pot and place over medium-high heat. After the garlic begins to sizzle, add the cooked broccoli. Season with pepper and lightly with salt and sauté for about 5 minutes. Stir periodically with a wooden spoon, using it to mash the broccoli into small pieces.
5. When the broccoli has finished sautéing, add 4 cups water and the bouillon cube and raise the heat to high. When the water begins boiling, add the pasta and cook covered over medium heat until the pasta is al dente. Serve hot.

TAGLIOLINI *in* BROTH

Tagliolini in Brodo

Few things warm the soul (and body) as well as these narrow egg noodles in a homemade meat broth. Of course a homemade broth takes more than 30 minutes to make, but I find it convenient to periodically make a batch and freeze it so that I'll always have some on hand. Here's a quick description of how to make it: put a chicken, some beef short ribs and perhaps brisket, some veal breast or bone-in shoulder, a peeled onion, celery, carrot, tomato, and a sprig of parsley in a stockpot. Season with salt and whole peppercorns, cover with cold water, and simmer, covered, for about three hours. When it is done, take the meat out, which is succulent and delicious, by the way, strain the broth, and freeze it in ice cube trays. When frozen, pop out the cubes and store in Ziploc bags. In the absence of homemade broth, use a good bouillon cube.

SERVES 4

5 cups homemade meat broth (see above) or ½ large beef bouillon cube and ½ large chicken bouillon cube dissolved in 5 cups water

4 ounces dried egg tagliolini or fettuccine

⅓ cup freshly grated Parmigiano-Reggiano

1. Put the broth in a soup pot and place over high heat. When the broth is boiling, add the tagliolini and stir until all the strands are submerged. When the broth comes back to a boil, lower the heat to medium and cook until al dente. Mix in the grated Parmigiano-Reggiano and serve at once.

CHILDREN'S PASTA SOUP

 Minestrina per i Bambini

I still remember how good this soup tasted when I was little and feeling under the weather. It felt so comforting and restorative. If your tummy isn't hurting, a little bit of butter mixed in gives the soup a richer flavor. Of course, a good homemade meat broth will make all the difference, but if you are fresh out, even made with a bouillon cube this soup will make you feel better. Use a combination of chicken and beef cubes to approximate the flavor of an Italian meat broth. See the previous recipe for a description of how to make Italian meat broth.

SERVES 4

1. Put the broth in a 3- to 4-quart soup pot, cover, and place over high heat. Once the broth is boiling, add the pasta. When the broth comes back to a boil, lower the heat and cook, covered, until the pasta is al dente. Remove from the heat, mix in the butter and grated Parmigiano-Reggiano, and serve at once.

5 cups Italian meat broth or ½ large beef bouillon cube and ½ large chicken bouillon cube dissolved in 5 cups water

6 ounces pastina (stars, alphabet pasta, or other small soup pasta shapes)

2 tablespoons butter (optional)

¼ cup freshly grated Parmigiano-Reggiano

VEGETARIAN
Pastas

Tagliatelle *with* Butter *and* Sage

Tagliatelle al Burro e Salvia

Sometimes the simplest sauces really are the best. This sauce is what is traditionally used with filled pastas such as tortelloni filled with spinach, Swiss chard, or ricotta and parsley. A good-quality egg pasta is essential here, the ideal, of course, being homemade.

SERVES 4

10–12 sprigs fresh sage

6 tablespoons butter

Salt

10 ounces dried egg tagliatelle (fettuccine or pappardelle are also good here)

½ cup freshly grated Parmigiano-Reggiano

1. Fill a pot for the pasta with about 6 quarts of water, place over high heat, and bring to a boil.
2. Coarsely chop the sage leaves. Put the butter and sage in a small saucepan, season with salt, and place over low heat. Remove from the heat as soon as the butter begins to brown.
3. When the water for the pasta is boiling, add about 2 tablespoons salt, add the tagliatelle, and stir until all the strands are submerged. Cook until al dente. When the pasta is done, drain well and toss with the butter and sage and the grated Parmigiano-Reggiano and serve at once.

Tagliolini *with* White Truffle

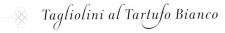

Tagliolini al Tartufo Bianco

Tagliolini are even narrower than fettuccine, optimizing the ratio of truffle to pasta. White truffles, particularly the ones from Alba in Piedmont, are much more intensely flavored than black truffles and, unfortunately, also much more expensive. Using truffle butter can be very good, but there is nothing like the flavor of thinly sliced fresh white truffles. Though they are expensive, do not skimp on the truffles in this recipe. Having it once with a generous portion of truffles is far better than several times with an insufficient one.

SERVES 4

1. Fill a pot for the pasta with about 6 quarts of water, place over high heat, and bring to a boil.
2. Melt the butter in a small saucepan over low heat, being careful not to let it brown. Add about 1 teaspoon salt and use a truffle slicer (or a peeler if you don't have one) to shave 8 to 10 slices of the truffle into the butter. Remove from the heat and set aside.
3. When the water for the pasta is boiling, add about 2 tablespoons salt, add the tagliolini, and stir until all the strands are submerged. Cook until al dente. When the pasta is done, drain well and transfer to a mixing bowl. Add the melted butter and the grated Parmigiano-Reggiano and toss well. Serve the pasta and shave the remaining truffle over each serving. Inhale deeply, and enjoy one of gastronomy's greatest pleasures!

6 tablespoons butter

Salt

2 ounces or more fresh white truffles

10 ounces dried egg tagliolini

¼ cup freshly grated Parmigiano-Reggiano

FETTUCCINE ALFREDO

Fettuccine alla Romana

Though much more common in America than in Italy, this dish did originate in Rome, where it was invented by the restaurant chef/owner Alfredo di Lelio. Actually, in Italy it is not known as Fettuccine Alfredo, but *Fettuccine alla Romana*, or simply *al burro e panna* (with butter and cream). It was discovered by Mary Pickford and Douglas Fairbanks when they visited his restaurant on their honeymoon in 1927. They were so enamored with the dish that they presented Alfredo with a gold-plated fork and spoon. It became his trademark to use those gold utensils to give his pasta a final toss before serving.

SERVES 4

3 tablespoons butter

1 cup heavy cream

¼ teaspoon freshly grated nutmeg

Salt

Freshly ground black pepper

½ cup freshly grated Parmigiano-Reggiano

10 ounces dried egg fettuccine

1. Fill a pot for the pasta with about 6 quarts of water, place over high heat, and bring to a boil.
2. Put the butter and heavy cream in a 12-inch skillet and place over medium-high heat. Add the nutmeg and season with salt and pepper. Cook until the sauce has thickened a bit and the cream has reduced by about one-third, about 2 minutes. Add the Parmigiano-Reggiano and stir until it is melted, then remove from the heat.
3. Add about 2 tablespoons salt to the boiling pasta water, add the fettuccine, and stir until all the strands are submerged. Cook until al dente.
4. When the pasta is done, drain well, transfer to the pan with the sauce, toss well, and serve at once.

FETTUCCINE *with* LEMON

Fettuccine al Limone

I have been making this elegant dish, with minor variations, since I learned it from my mother when I was a young man. I have never had a problem with the lemon curdling the cream, so I was surprised when a student of mine said it happened when she made it. It turns out she used half-and-half instead of cream. As long as you use heavy cream, you will not have to worry about curdling.

SERVES 4

1. Fill a pot for the pasta with about 6 quarts of water, place over high heat, and bring to a boil.
2. Finely grate the yellow peel of the lemon, taking care to avoid the bitter white pith. Squeeze the lemon with a juicer that will strain all the seeds. Put the butter, lemon juice, and zest in a 12-inch skillet and place over medium-high heat. As soon as the butter has melted, add the heavy cream and season with salt and pepper. Cook for about 2 minutes, until the cream has reduced by about one-third, then remove from the heat.
3. Add about 2 tablespoons salt to the boiling pasta water, add the fettuccine, and stir until all the strands are submerged. Cook until al dente.
4. When the pasta is done, drain well, transfer to the pan with the sauce, toss well with the grated Parmigiano-Reggiano, and serve at once.

1 lemon

3 tablespoons butter

1 cup heavy cream

Salt

Freshly ground black pepper

10 ounces dried egg fettuccine

⅔ cup freshly grated Parmigiano-Reggiano

FETTUCCINE *with* SPRING VEGETABLES

Fettuccine Primavera

This is such a popular dish that its Italian name almost does not need translation. A common mistake in making this is not sautéing the vegetables enough. Do not be afraid of overcooking them here. Whatever dubious virtue there may be in undercooking vegetables, it certainly does not apply to pasta sauces. By cutting the vegetables in tiny pieces and sautéing them thoroughly, you will concentrate their flavor and infuse the cream with it. Done properly, this is a heavenly dish with the rich, sweet flavors of spring.

SERVES 4

½ small yellow onion

1 large carrot

1 medium celery stalk

4 tablespoons butter

8 ounces asparagus

¾ red bell pepper

1½ medium zucchini (8 ounces)

1 cup heavy cream

4–5 sprigs flat-leaf Italian parsley

Salt

Freshly ground black pepper

½ cup freshly grated Parmigiano-Reggiano

10 ounces dried egg fettuccine

1. Peel and finely chop the onion. Peel the carrot and cut into ½-inch dice. Wash the celery, trim the top and bottom, and peel the back to remove the tough strings. Cut it into ¼-inch dice. Put the butter in a 12-inch skillet and place over medium-high heat. Once the butter begins to melt, add the onion, carrot, and celery and sauté until the vegetables begin to brown, about 5 minutes.

2. While the vegetables are sautéing, fill a 12-inch skillet with water and place over high heat. Cut off the white, woody bottom part of the asparagus spears, then peel the remaining bottom third. Add 1 teaspoon salt to the boiling water, then gently slide in the asparagus. Cook for 5 to 6 minutes or until the asparagus is tender, then lift them out and set aside.

3. Fill a pot for the pasta with about 6 quarts of water, place over high heat, and bring to a boil.

4. Wash the zucchini, trim the ends, and cut into ½-inch dice. Peel the pepper, core it and remove the seeds. Cut away any white pith inside the pepper and cut into 1-inch squares.

5. When the onion, carrot, and celery are ready, add the zucchini and peppers. Season generously with salt and pepper and continue sautéing until the zucchini and peppers are quite tender and lightly browned, about 15 minutes.

6. While the zucchini and peppers are cooking, finely chop enough parsley to measure 1½ tablespoons. Cut the cooked asparagus into pieces about 1 inch long. When the zucchini and peppers are ready, add the asparagus and sauté for about another minute. Add the cream and parsley and continue cooking until the cream has thickened and reduced by almost half.

7. While the cream is reducing, cook the pasta. Add about 2 tablespoons salt to the boiling pasta water, add the fettuccine, and stir until all the strands are submerged. Cook until al dente.

8. When the pasta is done, drain it well, toss with the sauce and the freshly grated Parmigiano-Reggiano, and serve at once.

SPAGHETTINI *with* FRESH HERBS

Spaghettini alle Erbe

Rosemary and thyme make this an intensely aromatic dish, with the parsley and basil rounding out the fragrance. Breadcrumbs soak up the flavors and cling to the pasta while providing a pleasing, crunchy texture. Use homemade breadcrumbs or the thicker panko-style crumbs.

SERVES 4

1 medium clove garlic

6–7 sprigs flat-leaf Italian parsley

1 sprig fresh rosemary

1–2 sprigs fresh thyme

Salt

1 pound spaghettini

6 tablespoons extra-virgin olive oil

7–8 fresh basil leaves

3 tablespoons breadcrumbs
(see above)

1. Fill a pot for the pasta with about 6 quarts of water, place over high heat, and bring to a boil.

2. Peel and finely chop the garlic. Chop enough parsley to measure 2 tablespoons, enough rosemary to measure ½ teaspoon, and enough thyme to measure 1 teaspoon.

3. When the water for the pasta is boiling, add about 2 tablespoons salt, add the spaghettini, and stir until all the strands are submerged. Cook until al dente.

4. While the pasta is cooking, put the olive oil, garlic, and parsley in an 8-inch skillet and place over medium heat. When the garlic is sizzling, add the rosemary and thyme. Season with salt and cook for about 1 minute. Shred the basil leaves and add them to the pan. Cook, stirring, for another 30 seconds, then remove from the heat.

5. When the pasta is done, drain well, toss with the sauce and the breadcrumbs, and serve at once.

SPAGHETTINI *with* OLIVE OIL *and* GARLIC

※ *Spaghettini all'Aglio e Olio*

If one had to choose a quintessential Italian pasta dish, this would definitely be at the top of the list. A favorite midnight snack in Rome, this pasta has often satisfied my late-night hunger cravings. Its few ingredients are likely already in your pantry, and its preparation is simple. It goes without saying that a very good extra-virgin olive oil is essential.

SERVES 4

1. Fill a pot for the pasta with about 6 quarts of water, place over high heat, and bring to a boil.
2. Peel and finely chop the garlic. Finely chop enough parsley to measure 1 tablespoon.
3. When the water for the pasta is boiling, add about 2 tablespoons salt, add the spaghettini, and stir until all the strands are submerged. Cook until al dente.
4. Put the garlic, hot red pepper flakes, olive oil, and parsley in an 8-inch skillet and place over medium-high heat. Season with salt. When the garlic begins to sizzle, cook for another 15 to 20 seconds, then remove from the heat. It's important not to let the garlic brown or it will become bitter.
5. When the pasta is done, drain well, toss with the sauce, and serve at once.

2 medium cloves garlic

3–4 sprigs flat-leaf Italian parsley

Salt

1 pound spaghettini

⅛ teaspoon hot red pepper flakes

6 tablespoons extra-virgin olive oil

Fettuccine *with* Gorgonzola

Fettuccine al Gorgonzola

Pasta with gorgonzola is a classic northern Italian dish that originated in Lombardy, where gorgonzola is made. Italian gorgonzola is not as sharp as many other blue cheeses and makes a delicious, richly flavored pasta sauce without being overpowering. Make sure to use the creamy gorgonzola dolce and not the sharper aged version.

SERVES 4

4 ounces Italian gorgonzola (see note above)

½ cup whole milk

2 tablespoons butter

Salt

¼ cup heavy cream

10 ounces dried egg fettuccine

⅓ cup freshly grated Parmigiano-Reggiano

1. Fill a pot for the pasta with about 6 quarts of water, place over high heat, and bring to a boil.
2. Put the gorgonzola, milk, and butter in a 12-inch skillet. Season with salt and place over medium heat. Cook, stirring constantly, until the cheese has melted completely. Add the cream, raise the heat to medium-high, and cook until the sauce has reduced and thickened, 2 to 3 minutes. Remove from the heat.
3. Add about 2 tablespoons salt to the boiling pasta water, add the fettuccine, and stir until all the strands are submerged. Cook until al dente.
4. When the pasta is done, drain well and transfer to the skillet. Add the freshly grated Parmigiano-Reggiano and toss the pasta thoroughly with the sauce. Serve at once.

SPAGHETTI *with* RAW PEPPERS *and* TOMATO

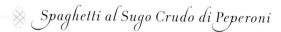
Spaghetti al Sugo Crudo di Peperoni

Saucing pasta with raw sauces is not uncommon and makes for a refreshing dish that minimizes your time spent in the kitchen. Some of these sauces require a period of maceration, but this one is best soon after it is made. The milk may seem like an odd ingredient but it softens the flavors and helps to blend them together. I remove the seeds from the tomatoes here so the sauce won't be too watery.

SERVES 4

1. Fill a pot for the pasta with about 6 quarts of water, place over high heat, and bring to a boil.
2. Peel the tomatoes and remove the seeds. Peel the pepper, core it, remove the seeds, and cut away any white pith inside. Roughly chop the pepper. Put the parsley, tomatoes, pepper, milk, 1½ teaspoons salt, and a light grinding of black pepper in a food processor. Pulse until you get a smooth puree.
3. When the water for the pasta is boiling, add about 2 tablespoons salt, add the spaghetti, and stir until all the strands are submerged. Cook until very al dente (about 30 seconds less than you normally would).
4. Transfer the sauce to the bowl where you will be serving the pasta. Add the Parmigiano-Reggiano and olive oil and mix well. When the pasta is done, drain well, toss thoroughly with the sauce, and let stand for about 2 minutes before serving.

1 pound fresh tomatoes

1 yellow bell pepper

3–4 sprigs flat-leaf Italian parsley

1 tablespoons whole milk

Salt

Freshly ground black pepper

1 pound spaghetti

¼ cup freshly grated Parmigiano-Reggiano

2 tablespoons extra-virgin olive oil

Tagliatelle *with* Peas

Tagliatelle ai Piselli

One of my favorite restaurants in Verona is Il Pompiere. They make a pasta dish when peas are in season that is thoroughly infused with their sweet flavor. Marco, the chef/owner, was kind enough to share his secret with me. It's actually very simple. Once the peas are tender, half are pureed until creamy and mixed back into the sauce. When the pasta is tossed with the sauce, it absorbs all that delicious pea flavor, which is why I like using the wider tagliatelle noodles. Although you could make this with premium frozen peas, the sweet flavor of fresh peas is worth the extra time it takes to shell them.

SERVES 4

1. Fill a pot for the pasta with about 6 quarts of water, place over high heat, and bring to a boil.

2. Peel and finely chop the onion. Put the olive oil in a saucepan or deep 8-inch skillet, add the chopped onion, and place over medium heat. Sauté until the onion turns a rich golden color, about 5 minutes.

3. While the onion is sautéing, shell the fresh peas, if using.

4. When the onion is ready, add the peas and season generously with salt and pepper. Stir the peas well, then add about ½ cup water. Cook over medium heat until the peas are tender, adding water if it evaporates completely before they are done. It should take 15 to 20 minutes for the peas to become tender. (If using frozen peas, add water only once and cook for 6 to 8 minutes).

5. When the peas are tender, remove from the heat, take out about half the peas, and puree them. A food mill will make the smoothest puree, but if you don't have one you can use a food processor. Put the pureed peas back in the pan with the whole peas.

6. Add about 2 tablespoons salt to the boiling pasta water, add the tagliatelle, and stir until all the strands are submerged. Cook until al dente.

7. After the pasta has cooked for about 2 minutes, add ¾ cup of the pasta water to the pan with the peas and stir well.

8. When the pasta is done, drain well, toss with the sauce, and serve at once.

½ medium yellow onion

4 tablespoons extra-virgin olive oil

1¾ pounds fresh peas
(or 12 ounces frozen peas)

Salt

Freshly ground black pepper

10 ounces dried egg tagliatelle or pappardelle

Linguine *with* Classic Basil Pesto

Linguine al Pesto di Basilico

Basil pesto is almost synonymous with Liguria, the Italian Riviera, and Genoa, its capital. What makes the pesto there unique is the tiny, fragrant sweet basil that grows in that region. Somehow, basil doesn't taste quite the same anywhere else. Purists would also insist that it be made by hand with a mortar and pestle. I have made a delicious pesto using American basil and a modern food processor, however, using the recipe below. In Liguria pesto is served with trenette, a flour-and-water pasta similar to linguine. It is also very good with spaghetti, spaghettini, or even potato gnocchi.

SERVES 4

1 small clove garlic

2 ounces basil (with stems)

⅓ cup pine nuts

Salt

6 tablespoons extra-virgin olive oil

¼ cup freshly grated Parmigiano-Reggiano

3 tablespoons freshly grated Pecorino Romano

1 pound linguine

1 tablespoon butter

1. Fill a pot for the pasta with about 6 quarts of water, place over high heat, and bring to a boil.

2. Peel the garlic. Put the basil leaves, garlic, pine nuts, 1¼ teaspoon salt, and olive oil in a food processor and pulse until the mixture is smooth. Transfer the contents to the bowl you'll be serving the pasta in and mix in the grated cheeses.

3. When the water for the pasta is boiling, add about 2 tablespoons salt to the boiling pasta water, add the linguine, and stir until all the strands are submerged. Cook until al dente. When the pasta is about halfway done, add two tablespoons of the pasta water and the butter to the pesto and mix well. When the pasta is done, drain well, toss vigorously until it is well coated with the pesto, and serve at once.

NOTE: Pesto can be made ahead of time and frozen for up to 2 months. After adding the cheeses, place the pesto in a freezer-safe container and coat the surface with olive oil before sealing and placing in the freezer. Defrost before adding the pasta water and butter.

SPAGHETTI *with* CREAMY BASIL PESTO

Spaghetti al Pesto Ligure con Quagliata

The first basil pesto recipe is thought to be from the mid-eighteenth century, though the word *pesto* implies any sauce that is *pestato,* or mashed, traditionally in a marble mortar and pestle. Its origins may be from the Orient, where sauces of pine nuts and cheese mashed together were the custom. The most common version is with Parmigiano-Reggiano and aged pecorino cheese, as in the previous recipe. A lesser-known traditional recipe has no pecorino but instead uses a cheese curd called *quagliata* in Italian. Its closest readily available equivalent is ricotta, and it makes a richer, creamier pesto. Though this is sacrilegious to purists, I have no problem making it in a food processor. It's best to use the pulsing action to avoid "cooking" the basil by running the processor too long and overheating it.

SERVES 4

1. Fill a pot for the pasta with about 6 quarts of water, place over high heat, and bring to a boil.
2. Peel the garlic. Put the basil leaves, garlic, pine nuts, 1¼ teaspoons salt, and olive oil in a food processor and pulse until the mixture is smooth.
3. When the water for the pasta is boiling, add about 2 tablespoons salt, add the spaghetti, and stir until all the strands are submerged. Cook until al dente.
4. Transfer the basil mixture to a serving bowl and mix in the Parmigiano-Reggiano and ricotta. When the pasta is about halfway done, add 2 tablespoons of the pasta water and mix well.
5. When the pasta is done, drain well, toss with the pesto in the bowl, and serve at once.

2 medium cloves garlic

2 ounces basil (with stems)

2 tablespoons pine nuts

Salt

5 tablespoons extra-virgin olive oil

1 pound spaghetti (linguine is also good here)

⅓ cup freshly grated Parmigiano-Reggiano

¼ cup whole-milk ricotta

Spaghetti *with* Walnut Pesto

Spaghetti al Pesto di Noci

In Liguria, the Italian Riviera, walnut pesto is almost as common as basil pesto. This is one of several equally good variations I have tried, and is best suited to sturdier flour-and-water pasta. The bread soaked in milk adds creaminess and body to the sauce.

SERVES 4

1 slice white bread

¼ cup whole milk

1 small clove garlic

4 ounces shelled walnuts

1–2 sprigs fresh oregano (about 1 teaspoon tightly packed leaves)

3 tablespoons extra-virgin olive oil

Salt

1 pound spaghetti

1. Fill a pot for the pasta with about 6 quarts of water, place over high heat, and bring to a boil.
2. Remove the crust from the slice of bread and discard. Put the bread in a shallow bowl with the milk.
3. Peel the garlic and put it in a food processor with the walnuts, oregano, olive oil, and 1 teaspoon salt. Add the bread-and-milk mixture and pulse until you obtain a smooth, creamy consistency. Transfer the pesto to the bowl you will be serving the pasta in.
4. Add about 2 tablespoons salt to the boiling pasta water, put in the spaghetti, and stir until all the strands are submerged. Cook until al dente. When the pasta is about halfway done, add about ¼ cup of the pasta water to the pesto in the bowl and mix it in well. When the pasta is done, drain well, toss with the sauce, and serve at once.

LINGUINE *with* PARSLEY *and* MINT PESTO

A pesto can be anything that is mashed to a pulp with a mortar and pestle. Basil pesto is the best known, but there are several other kinds of pesto that can be used as a pasta sauce. This is a particularly fragrant and refreshing one.

SERVES 4

1. Fill a pot for the pasta with about 6 quarts of water, place over high heat, and bring to a boil.
2. Put the parsley, mint, pine nuts, olive oil and 1¼ teaspoons salt in a food processor. Pulse until the mixture is smooth.
3. Add about 2 tablespoons salt to the boiling pasta water, add the linguine, and stir until all the strands are submerged. Cook until al dente.
4. While the pasta is cooking, transfer the mixture from the food processor to a serving bowl. Grate the pecorino cheese and mix it into the pesto. When the pasta is about halfway done, add about 2 tablespoons of the pasta water and mix well.
5. When the pasta is done, drain well, toss with the pesto in the bowl, and serve at once.

24 sprigs flat-leaf Italian parsley (about ½ cup of loosely packed leaves)

10–12 sprigs fresh mint (about ⅓ cup loosely packed leaves)

½ cup pine nuts

5 tablespoons extra-virgin olive oil

Salt

1 pound linguine

3 ounces pecorino cheese (use a medium-aged cheese such as Crosta Rossa di Pienza, not aged Pecorino Romano)

TAGLIATELLE *with* CHICKPEAS

Tagliatelle coi Ceci

One of the restaurants we enjoy going to when we are in Valpolicella, the wine country outside of Verona, is Alla Rosa Alda, in the tiny hilltop town of San Giorgio. One of their specialties is a pasta dish they call "Tagliatelle Embogonè" in the local dialect. It is homemade egg noodles with a sauce of fresh cranberry beans. When I was growing up, my mother made a soup with chickpeas, tomatoes, and rosemary that I loved. I've adapted it here, taking inspiration from Alla Rosa Alda's dish, into a pasta sauce that is now one of our favorites at home.

SERVES 4

½ medium yellow onion

3 tablespoons extra-virgin olive oil, plus a little extra for drizzling at the end

1 medium clove garlic

1–2 sprigs fresh rosemary

1 pound fresh tomatoes

Salt

1½ cups canned chickpeas, drained

Freshly ground black pepper

10 ounces dried egg tagliatelle

1. Fill a pot for the pasta with about 6 quarts of water, place over high heat, and bring to a boil.
2. Peel the onion and finely chop it. Put it and the olive oil in a 12-inch skillet and place over medium-high heat. Sauté until the onion turns a rich golden color, about 5 minutes.
3. While the onion is sautéing, peel the garlic and finely chop it. Finely chop enough rosemary to measure 1 teaspoon. Peel the tomatoes and coarsely chop them.
4. When the onion is ready, add the garlic and rosemary. Sauté for 10 to 15 seconds, then add the tomatoes. Season lightly with salt and cook until most of the liquid the tomatoes release has evaporated, about 10 minutes. Add the chickpeas, season with pepper and again lightly with salt, and cook for 5 more minutes. Scoop out about half the chickpeas and puree them. A food mill will produce a smoother texture, but if you don't have one you can use a food processor. Mix the pureed chickpeas into the sauce and cook for another 1 to 2 minutes.
5. Once the pureed chickpeas are back in the pan, add about 2 tablespoons salt to the boiling pasta water, add the tagliatelle, and stir until all the strands are submerged. Cook until al dente.
6. After the pasta has cooked about 2 minutes, mix 2 tablespoons of the pasta water into the sauce. When the pasta is done, drain well and toss with the sauce. Drizzle a little olive oil and grind some black pepper over each portion and serve at once.

SPAGHETTI *with* RAW TOMATOES, HERBS, *and* MOZZARELLA

Spaghetti alla Checca

I discovered this classic, refreshing Neapolitan summer dish at a restaurant called Cambusa in Positano. It is an uncooked sauce in which the ingredients are simply scalded with hot oil before being tossed with the pasta, releasing the bright flavors. The mozzarella is tossed with the hot pasta at the end, then the dish stands briefly before serving so that the cheese melts slightly.

SERVES 4

2 pounds fresh tomatoes

Salt

1 pound spaghetti

6 tablespoons extra-virgin olive oil

8 ounces fresh whole-milk mozzarella

6–8 fresh basil leaves

4–5 sprigs fresh oregano

3–4 sprigs fresh thyme

Freshly ground black pepper

1. Fill a pot for the pasta with about 6 quarts of water, place over high heat, and bring to a boil.
2. Peel the tomatoes, remove the seeds, and cut into small ¼-inch dice. Put the tomatoes in the serving bowl you'll be serving the pasta in.
3. When the water for the pasta is boiling, add about 2 tablespoons salt, add the spaghetti, and stir until all the strands are submerged. Cook until very al dente (about 30 seconds less than you normally would).
4. While the pasta is cooking, put the olive oil in a small saucepan and place over medium heat. Heat until the oil just begins to smoke, then remove from the heat.
5. While the oil is heating, cut the mozzarella into ¼-inch dice. Coarsely chop the basil. Finely chop enough oregano to measure about 4 teaspoons and enough thyme to measure about 1 teaspoon. Add the herbs to the bowl with the tomatoes and season well with salt and pepper. Pour the hot oil into the bowl with the herbs and mix thoroughly.
6. When the pasta is done, drain well and toss it with the ingredients in the serving bowl. Add the mozzarella, toss again, then cover the bowl and let stand for about a minute to allow the cheese to melt a bit. Uncover the bowl, toss one last time, and serve at once.

Spaghetti *with a* Raw Tomato Sauce

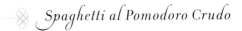 *Spaghetti al Pomodoro Crudo*

It always surprises me how good a raw tomato sauce for pasta can be. It has a simple, fresh flavor that makes it an ideal summer dish. As in the previous recipe, since the tomatoes are used raw, the best ripe, flavorful tomatoes and a very good olive oil are essential.

SERVES 4

1. Fill a pot for the pasta with about 6 quarts of water, place over high heat, and bring to a boil.
2. Peel the tomatoes, remove the seeds, and cut into small ¼-inch dice. Put them in the bowl you will be serving the pasta in. Peel and lightly crush the garlic cloves and add them to the bowl. Finely chop enough parsley to measure 2 tablespoons and add it to the bowl. Coarsely chop the basil and mix into the rest of the ingredients in the bowl.
3. When the water for the pasta is boiling, add about 2 tablespoons salt, add the spaghetti, and stir until all the strands are submerged. Cook until al dente.
4. When the pasta is almost done, add 1½ teaspoons salt and the olive oil to the sauce in the bowl and mix well. When the pasta is done, drain well, toss with the sauce, and serve at once.

2 pounds fresh tomatoes

2 medium cloves garlic

6–7 sprigs flat-leaf Italian parsley

12–14 fresh basil leaves

Salt

1 pound spaghetti

4 tablespoons extra-virgin olive oil

Spaghettini *with* Fresh Tomato, Olive Oil, *and* Basil

Spaghettini al Pomodoro e Basilico

This is the quintessential *pasta al pomodoro*. It has the sweet flavor of fresh tomatoes highlighted by a hint of hot red pepper, not to make the sauce spicy but to give it a little liveliness. Although the amount of garlic may seem excessive, as it stews with the tomatoes it becomes quite mild, making the sauce rich rather than pungent. The key is allowing the garlic to sizzle for only a few seconds before adding the tomatoes.

SERVES 4

2½ pounds fresh, ripe tomatoes

5–6 medium cloves garlic

4 tablespoons extra-virgin olive oil

⅛ teaspoon hot red pepper flakes

Salt

10–12 fresh basil leaves

1 pound spaghettini

1. Fill a pot for the pasta with about 6 quarts of water, place over high heat, and bring to a boil.
2. Peel the tomatoes and cut into ½-inch dice.
3. Peel and thinly slice the garlic. Put the garlic, 3 tablespoons of the olive oil, and the hot red pepper flakes in a 12-inch skillet and place over high heat. The moment the garlic begins to sizzle, add the tomatoes and season generously with salt. Cook for about 15 minutes, stirring occasionally, until most of the liquid from the tomatoes has evaporated. Coarsely shred the basil and add to the sauce. Continue cooking until all the liquid in the pan has evaporated.
4. After adding the basil, add 2 tablespoons salt to the boiling pasta water, add the spaghettini, and stir until all the strands are submerged. Cook until al dente.
5. When the pasta is done, drain well, toss with the sauce and the remaining tablespoon olive oil, and serve at once.

PENNE *with* PEPPERS, FRESH TOMATO, *and* BASIL

 Penne ai Peperoni e Pomodoro Fresco

I often make a risotto with red and yellow peppers, tomatoes, and basil whose enticing colors and aroma make it one of my family's favorites. As a pasta dish, with its fresh and fragrant combination of flavors, it becomes a great light summer meal.

SERVES 8

1. Fill a pot for the pasta with about 6 quarts of water, place over high heat, and bring to a boil.

2. Peel and finely chop the onion. Put it with the butter in a 12-inch skillet and place over medium heat. Sauté until the onion turns a rich golden color, about 5 minutes.

3. While the onion is sautéing, peel the peppers, core, and seed them. Cut away any white pith inside the peppers and cut into 1-inch squares. When the onion is ready, add the peppers and season lightly with salt. Raise the heat to medium-high and sauté until they are mostly tender and begin to brown lightly, about 10 minutes.

4. While the peppers are cooking, peel the tomatoes and coarsely chop them. When the peppers are ready, add the tomatoes and season lightly with salt. Cook until the tomatoes have reduced and the liquid the tomatoes release has evaporated, about 10 more minutes.

5. After the tomatoes have cooked for about 5 minutes, coarsely chop the basil and add it to the pan. Add about 2 tablespoons salt to the boiling pasta water, add the penne, and stir well. Cook until al dente.

6. When the pasta is done, drain well, toss with the sauce and the Parmigiano-Reggiano, and serve at once.

½ medium yellow onion

3 tablespoons butter

1 red bell pepper

1 yellow bell pepper

Salt

1½ pounds fresh, ripe tomatoes

1 pound penne (fusilli or a wide egg noodle such as pappardelle or tagliatelle are also good)

8–10 fresh basil leaves

⅓ cup freshly grated Parmigiano-Reggiano

FUSILLI *with a* RAINBOW-COLORED SAUCE

Fusilli Arcobaleno

In truth, this is not one of the recipes that exemplifies the few-ingredient style of Italian cooking. What *is* very Italian is how the ingredients do not all blend into one another—you can taste the flavor of each one. The amount of preparation is also not as daunting as it might seem, because the amounts are small and the vegetables are added in stages, so you can work as the sauce cooks. I also add the salt in stages here, seasoning each ingredient as it goes in, to best bring out the flavor.

SERVES 4

½ small yellow onion

3 tablespoons extra-virgin olive oil

1 medium clove garlic

½ green bell pepper

½ yellow bell pepper

⅛ teaspoon hot red pepper flakes

Salt

1 medium zucchini (6–7 ounces)

¾ pound fresh tomatoes

½ medium eggplant (8 ounces)

1 pound fusilli

½ cup packed arugula (about 1 ounce)

8–10 fresh basil leaves

1. Fill a pot for the pasta with about 6 quarts of water, place over high heat, and bring to a boil.
2. Peel the onion and finely chop it. Put the olive oil in a 12-inch skillet, add the chopped onion, and place over medium-high heat. Sauté until the onion turns a rich golden color, about 5 minutes.
3. While the onion is sautéing, peel and finely chop the garlic. Peel the green and yellow peppers and cut them into ¼-inch dice.
4. When the onion is ready, add the garlic, peppers, and hot red pepper flakes. Lightly season with salt and continue sautéing over medium-high heat for about 3 minutes, stirring periodically.
5. While the peppers are sautéing, wash the zucchini, trim the ends, and cut into chunks no bigger than ½ inch. Add them to the pan and season them lightly with salt. Continue cooking until the zucchini is almost tender, 6 to 8 minutes.
6. While the zucchini is cooking, peel the tomatoes and coarsely chop them. Peel the eggplant and cut it into ½-inch cubes.
7. When the zucchini is ready, add the tomatoes and eggplant and season lightly with salt. Cover the pan, lower the heat to medium, and cook until the eggplant is tender and becomes translucent, 8 to 10 minutes.
8. When the eggplant is halfway done, add about 2 tablespoons salt to the boiling pasta water, add the fusilli, and stir well. Cook until al dente.
9. Wash the arugula and coarsely chop the basil. When the eggplant is tender, uncover the pan and add the arugula and basil. Continue cooking until the arugula has wilted completely, 1 to 2 minutes, then remove from the heat.
10. When the pasta is done, drain well, toss with the sauce, and serve at once.

Spaghetti *with* Tomato *and* Bay Leaves

Spaghetti al Pomodoro e Alloro

The addition of bay leaves gives this basic tomato sauce a distinctive herbal flavor. Both butter and olive oil are used here, which is unusual. The flavor of bay leaves goes well with olive oil, while the butter makes the sauce mellower.

SERVES 4

1 medium sweet yellow onion

2 tablespoons extra-virgin olive oil

2 tablespoons butter

Salt

2 pounds fresh tomatoes

4 dried bay leaves (or fresh, if available)

Freshly ground black pepper

1 pound spaghetti (penne or maccheroni are also good)

⅓ cup freshly grated Parmigiano-Reggiano

1. Fill a pot for the pasta with about 6 quarts of water, place over high heat, and bring to a boil.
2. Peel the onion and slice thinly crosswise. Put it with the olive oil and butter in a 12-inch skillet. Place over medium-high heat, season lightly with salt, and sauté until the onion turns a rich golden color, 6 to 8 minutes.
3. While the onion is sautéing, peel the tomatoes and coarsely chop them.
4. When the onion is ready, add the tomatoes and bay leaves, season with salt and pepper, and cook until the liquid the tomatoes release has almost completely evaporated, 10 to 12 minutes. Remove from the heat.
5. After the tomatoes have been cooking for about 8 minutes, add about 2 tablespoons salt to the boiling pasta water, add the spaghetti, and stir until all the strands are submerged. Cook until al dente.
6. When the pasta is done, drain well, toss with the sauce and Parmigiano-Reggiano, and serve at once.

Spaghettini *with* Tomatoes *and* Olives

 *Spaghettini alle Olive*

This is a little like the classic Puttanesca sauce (page 123) but without the anchovies and capers and with parsley instead of oregano. I love its clean and direct flavor and, although it is good with spaghetti, I particularly like it with the thinner spaghettini.

SERVES 4

1. Fill a pot for the pasta with about 6 quarts of water, place over high heat, and bring to a boil.
2. Peel the tomatoes and coarsely chop them.
3. Peel the garlic and finely chop it. Finely chop enough parsley to measure about 2 tablespoons. Put the garlic, parsley, and olive oil in a 12-inch skillet and place over medium-high heat. When the garlic is sizzling, add the tomatoes. Season with salt and cook until the liquid the tomatoes released has evaporated, 10 to 12 minutes.
4. While the tomatoes are cooking, slice the flesh of the olives away from the pits into slivers. When the tomatoes are almost ready, add about 2 tablespoons salt to the boiling pasta water, add the spaghettini, and stir until all the strands are submerged. Cook until al dente.
5. When the tomatoes are ready, add the olives, cook for 1 to 2 more minutes, then remove from the heat.
6. When the pasta is done, drain well, toss with the sauce, and serve at once.

2 pounds fresh tomatoes

1 large clove garlic

6–7 sprigs flat-leaf Italian parsley

4 tablespoons extra-virgin olive oil

Salt

16 Kalamata olives

1 pound spaghettini

Spaghettini *with* Eggplant

Spaghettini alle Melanzane

Eggplant and tomatoes seem made for each other, and this is an easy sauce that I particularly like to serve with spaghettini. A word of caution, however: when using spaghettini it's essential to use a premium brand, or the pasta may break up when you toss it with the sauce. If a high-quality pasta is not available, use spaghetti instead.

SERVES 4

1 medium yellow onion

4 tablespoons extra-virgin olive oil

1 medium clove garlic

1 pound fresh tomatoes

1 medium eggplant
(about 1 pound)

Salt

8–10 fresh basil leaves

1 pound spaghettini (or spaghetti;
see note above)

1. Fill a pot for the pasta with about 6 quarts of water, place over high heat, and bring to a boil.
2. Peel the onion and thinly slice it crosswise. Put it with 3 tablespoons of the olive oil in a 12-inch skillet over medium-high heat and sauté until the onion turns a rich golden color, 6 to 8 minutes.
3. While the onion is sautéing, peel the garlic and finely chop it. Peel the tomatoes and coarsely chop them. Trim the ends of the eggplant, peel it, and cut it into 1/2-inch chunks.
4. When the onion is ready, add the garlic and sauté for 10 to 15 seconds. Add the tomatoes and the eggplant and season with salt. Cover the pan and cook until the eggplant is tender, 10 to 12 minutes.
5. While the eggplant and tomatoes are cooking, shred the basil. When the eggplant is tender, uncover the pan, add the basil, and continue cooking until the liquid in the pan has almost completely evaporated.
6. After uncovering the pan, add about 2 tablespoons salt to the boiling pasta water, add the spaghettini, and stir until all the strands are submerged. Cook until al dente.
7. When the pasta is done, drain well, toss with the sauce and the remaining tablespoon of olive oil, and serve at once.

PENNE *with* LEEKS, ZUCCHINI, *and* PEPPERS

Penne ai Porri, Zucchine e Peperoni

Occasionally, inspiration hits when you just open the refrigerator door and see what's inside. This is one of those happy instances, and my family decreed the recipe "must go in the book!" The leeks give the sauce a sweet, rich flavor that is nicely balanced by the tanginess of the red pepper.

SERVES 4

1. Fill a pot for the pasta with about 6 quarts of water, place over high heat, and bring to a boil.
2. Cut off the root end of the leeks and trim the tough dark-green tops of the leaves. Cut into thin strips about 1½ inches long. Put the leeks in a bowl and cover with water. Swish them around to remove any dirt, then lift them out and put them with the butter and ½ cup water in a 12-inch skillet. Season with salt and place over medium-high heat. Cook, covered, until wilted, about 5 minutes. Uncover and continue cooking until the liquid in the pan has evaporated.
3. While the leeks are cooking, peel the pepper, core, and seed it. Cut away any white pith inside the pepper and cut into ½-inch squares. Wash the zucchini, trim the ends, and cut into ½-inch chunks.
4. Once the liquid in the pan has evaporated, add the peppers and zucchini. Season with salt and pepper, and cook until tender and lightly browned, about 15 minutes. If the vegetables begin to stick to the pan before they are tender, add a couple tablespoons of water.
5. Add about two tablespoons salt to the boiling pasta water, add the penne, and stir well. Cook until al dente.
6. While the pasta is cooking, add the cream to the vegetables and cook, stirring, for about 1 minute, then remove from the heat.
7. When the pasta is done, drain well, toss with the sauce and the Parmigiano-Reggiano, and serve at once.

2 medium leeks

3 tablespoons butter

Salt

1 red bell pepper

¾ pound zucchini

Freshly ground black pepper

1 pound penne

⅓ cup heavy cream

⅓ cup freshly grated Parmigiano-Reggiano

SPAGHETTI *with* CHEESE *and* PEPPER

Spaghetti al Cacio e Pepe

Johann Wolfgang von Goethe published an account of his travels in Italy between 1786 and 1788, called *Italian Journey*. In it he writes of the pasta he encountered in Naples: "As a rule, it is simply cooked in water and seasoned with grated cheese." This is, in fact, the prevalent way that pasta used to be served in southern Italy. Today the dish has become a Roman specialty. Some people swear that it must be made with the sharper aged Pecorino Romano, while others insist a younger pecorino is called for. I personally like using a medium-aged pecorino, which melts more easily and is better suited to the generous amount of black pepper used here.

SERVES 4

2 tablespoons extra-virgin olive oil

Salt

½ teaspoon freshly ground black pepper

½ pound pecorino cheese (use a medium-aged cheese such as Crosta Rossa di Pienza)

1 pound spaghetti

1. Fill a pot for the pasta with about 6 quarts of water, place over high heat, and bring to a boil.
2. Put the olive oil, 1¼ teaspoons salt, and pepper in a small saucepan and place over very low heat.
3. Grate the cheese using the medium-sized holes of a grater and put it in the bowl you'll be serving the pasta in.
4. When the water for the pasta is boiling, add about 2 tablespoons salt, add the spaghetti, and stir until all the strands are submerged. Cook until al dente.
5. A few minutes before the pasta is ready, add ¼ cup of the pasta water to the bowl with the cheese. Stir vigorously until a creamy paste is formed. When the pasta is ready, drain well and transfer to the serving bowl. Toss very well until the pasta is coated with the cheese. Add the hot olive oil with the salt and pepper, toss again, and serve at once.

PENNE *with* MUSHROOMS *and* ZUCCHINI

Penne ai Funghi e Zucchine

Here is a fresh and tasty combination. Zucchini makes this a lighter, fresher sauce than one with just mushrooms. A small amount of fresh tomatoes helps to bind the vegetables into a cohesive sauce. In addition to penne, I like this with shapes that have ridges or cavities to catch the sauce.

SERVES 4

¾ **pound zucchini**

2 **medium cloves garlic**

3 **tablespoons extra-virgin olive oil**

Salt

½ **pound white mushrooms**

Freshly ground black pepper

½ **pound fresh tomatoes**

1 **pound penne**

2–3 **sprigs fresh thyme**

1. Fill a pot for the pasta with about 6 quarts of water, place over high heat, and bring to a boil.
2. Wash the zucchini, trim the ends, and cut into ½-inch chunks. Peel the garlic, thinly slice it, and put it with the olive oil in a 12-inch skillet. Place over medium-high heat. When the garlic begins to sizzle, add the zucchini, season lightly with salt, and sauté, stirring often, until the zucchini starts becoming tender and lightly browned, about 5 minutes.
3. While the zucchini is cooking, brush away any dirt from the fresh mushrooms and thinly slice them. When the zucchini is ready, add the mushrooms and season with pepper and lightly with salt. Cook until the liquid released has evaporated, 4 to 5 minutes.
4. While the mushrooms are cooking, peel the tomatoes and coarsely chop them.
5. When the mushrooms are ready, add about 2 tablespoons salt to the boiling pasta water, add the penne, and stir well. Cook until al dente.
6. Reduce the heat under the sauce to medium, add the tomatoes, and season lightly with salt. Chop enough of the thyme leaves to measure 1 teaspoon and add them to the pan. Cook until the liquid the tomatoes release has reduced, 3 to 4 minutes, then remove from the heat.
7. When the pasta is done, drain well, toss with the sauce, and serve at once.

Spaghetti *with* Melon

Spaghetti al Melone

I remember eating with my parents many years ago at a restaurant in Venice that specialized in unusual dishes, none of which were seafood or risotto, the staples of Venetian cuisine. The restaurant is no longer there, and I don't remember its name, but I do remember this delicious dish of pasta with cantaloupe. Its flavor is rich and almost tangy—not as sweet as one might imagine. My mother started making it at home, and now I often make it when we have friends over. Once it is cooked, the melon is mostly unrecognizable, and it's great fun seeing if people can guess what the sauce's secret ingredient is.

SERVES 4

1. Fill a pot for the pasta with about 6 quarts of water, place over high heat, and bring to a boil.
2. Cut away the rind of the melon down to the orange flesh. Cut the melon in half, discard the seeds, and cut the melon into ½-inch dice. Put the butter in a 12-inch skillet and place over medium-high heat. Once the butter has melted completely, add the melon and season generously with salt and pepper. Cook, stirring often, until the melon begins to break down and most of the liquid it releases has evaporated, about 10 minutes.
3. Add about 2 tablespoons salt to the boiling pasta water, add the spaghetti, and stir until all the strands are submerged. Cook until al dente.
4. Add the tomato paste and lemon juice to the melon and stir well. Add the cream and cook until the sauce thickens and reduces by about a third, 2 to 3 minutes. Remove from the heat.
5. When the pasta is done, drain well, toss with the sauce and the Parmigiano-Reggiano, and serve at once.

1 3-pound cantaloupe

3 tablespoons butter

Salt

Freshly ground black pepper

1 pound spaghetti (linguine is also good)

2 teaspoons tomato paste

1½ teaspoons freshly squeezed lemon juice

½ cup heavy cream

½ cup freshly grated Parmigiano-Reggiano

Fusilli *with* Green *and* Yellow Peppers

Fusilli con la Peperonata

A peperonata is a classic sauce of stewed peppers and tomatoes that is traditionally served with mixed boiled meats, and sometimes also as a side dish. I've found that this adaptation makes a terrific pasta sauce, too. I like using green peppers, whose tartness balances the sweetness of the yellow peppers. Although Parmigiano-Reggiano is not ordinarily used with an olive oil–based sauce, I sometimes like to add just a little for flavor.

SERVES 4

½ large sweet yellow onion

3 tablespoons extra-virgin olive oil

⅛ teaspoon hot red pepper flakes

1 medium clove garlic

1 green bell pepper

1 yellow bell pepper

Salt

1 pound fresh tomatoes

1 pound fusilli

2 sprigs fresh oregano

¼ cup freshly grated Parmigiano-Reggiano (optional)

1. Fill a pot for the pasta with about 6 quarts of water, place over high heat, and bring to a boil.

2. Peel the onion and thinly slice it crosswise. Put it with the olive oil and hot red pepper flakes in a 12-inch skillet and place over medium heat. Sauté until the onion turns a rich golden color, 6 to 8 minutes.

3. While the onion is sautéing, peel and thinly slice the garlic. Peel the peppers, core, and seed them. Cut away any white pith inside the peppers and cut them into strips about 1 inch long and ½ inch wide. When the onions are ready, raise the heat to medium-high, add the garlic, stir for about 10 seconds, then add the peppers. Season with salt and cook until they are almost tender and begin to brown lightly, about 10 minutes.

4. While the peppers are cooking, peel the tomatoes and coarsely chop them. When the peppers are ready, add the tomato, season lightly with salt, and continue cooking until the liquid the tomatoes release is almost completely reduced, 6 to 8 minutes.

5. While the tomatoes are cooking, add about 2 tablespoons salt to the boiling pasta water, add the fusilli, and stir well. Cook until al dente.

6. While the pasta is cooking, chop enough oregano to measure 1 teaspoon and add it to the sauce.

7. When the pasta is done, drain well, toss with the sauce and the grated Parmigiano-Reggiano, if desired, and serve at once.

Fusilli *with* Leeks *and* Red Onions

 Fusilli ai Porri e Cipolla Rossa

Leeks are onions' milder cousins, and when they cook down they become sweet and creamy. Red onions add depth of flavor, making this a perfect pasta sauce for when the weather starts turning cold.

SERVES 4

1. Fill a pot for the pasta with about 6 quarts of water, place over high heat, and bring to a boil.

2. Peel and thinly slice the red onion crosswise. Put it with the olive oil in a 12-inch skillet and place over medium-high heat. Sauté the onion while you are preparing the leeks. If the onion begins to brown, remove from the heat.

3. While the onion is sautéing, cut off the root ends of the leeks and trim the tough dark-green tops of the leaves. Cut the leeks into narrow strips 2 to 3 inches long, put them in a bowl, and cover with water. Swish the leeks with your hands to remove any dirt. Lift the leeks out of the water in the bowl and add them to the pan. Season with salt and pepper and add about ½ cup of water. Cover the pan, lower the heat to medium, and cook until the leeks are very tender, about 15 minutes. Check them periodically and add more water if the liquid evaporates before they are done.

4. While the leeks are cooking, finely chop enough parsley to measure about 2 tablespoons.

5. After the leeks have cooked for 15 minutes, add about 2 tablespoons salt to the boiling pasta water, add the fusilli, and stir well. Cook until al dente.

6. When the leeks are done, uncover the pan, and if there is still liquid in the pan, raise the heat until the liquid is almost completely evaporated. If the pan is completely dry, add about ¼ cup of the pasta water to moisten. Stir in the parsley and cook for another minute.

7. When the pasta is ready, drain well, toss with the sauce and the grated Parmigiano-Reggiano, and serve at once.

1 medium red onion

4 tablespoons extra-virgin olive oil

2 medium leeks

Salt

Freshly ground black pepper

6–7 sprigs flat-leaf Italian parsley

1 pound fusilli (spaghetti is also good)

½ cup freshly grated Parmigiano-Reggiano

FUSILLI *with* BROCCOFLOWER

 Fusilli al Cavolo Romanesco

Broccoflower, which looks somewhat like a green cauliflower, has a wonderfully sweet, nutty flavor and makes a delicious pasta sauce. It's important to season it aggressively in order for its flavor to come through and in order to properly season the pasta.

SERVES 4

1. Fill a pot large enough to comfortably hold the broccoflower with water, place over high heat, and bring to a boil.

2. Fill a pot for the pasta with about 6 quarts of water, place over high heat, and bring to a boil.

3. Remove the leaves around the broccoflower and cut off the root. Peel and finely chop the garlic cloves. Grate the pecorino cheese.

4. When the water for the broccoflower is boiling, add 1 tablespoon salt and add the broccoflower. Cook until tender, 10 to 12 minutes, then remove it from the boiling water and transfer to a cutting board. Chop the cooked broccoflower into $1/2$-inch chunks.

5. Add 2 tablespoons salt to the boiling pasta water, add the fusilli, and stir well. Cook until al dente.

6. While the pasta is cooking, put the chopped garlic, hot red pepper flakes, and 4 tablespoons of the olive oil in a 12-inch skillet and place over medium-high heat. When the garlic is sizzling, add the chopped broccoflower, season generously with salt, and sauté over medium heat, stirring periodically, until the pasta is done. If the broccoflower begins to stick on the bottom of the skillet, add a little bit of the boiling pasta water.

7. When the fusilli are done, drain well, toss with the sauce, the remaining tablespoon olive oil, and the grated pecorino cheese, and serve at once.

1 broccoflower

2 medium cloves garlic

2 ounces medium-aged pecorino cheese (such as Crosta Rossa di Pienza)

Salt

1 pound fusilli

1/4 teaspoon hot red pepper flakes

5 tablespoons extra-virgin olive oil

Fusilli *with* Roasted Peppers

Fusilli ai Peperoni Arrosto

Roasting peppers gives them a distinctively rich flavor that is well suited to savory capers and Romano cheese. There are several ways to roast peppers. The quickest is over the open flame of a gas burner. Another way is on a barbecue grill. Alternatively, you can do it under the broiler of your oven. Once they are roasted, put them in a plastic bag and tie it shut. The steam that is trapped inside will lift the skin, making peeling them a snap.

SERVES 4

1 yellow (or red) bell pepper

1 green bell pepper

1 pound fresh tomatoes

2 medium cloves garlic

3 tablespoons extra-virgin olive oil

Salt

1 pound fusilli

Freshly ground black pepper

3–4 sprigs flat-leaf Italian parsley

1 tablespoon capers

¼ cup freshly grated Pecorino Romano cheese

1. Fill a pot for the pasta with about 6 quarts of water, place over high heat, and bring to a boil.
2. Roast the peppers until most of the skin is charred, then place in a plastic bag and tie it shut to trap the steam inside.
3. Peel the tomatoes and coarsely chop them.
4. Peel and lightly crush the garlic cloves. Put them with the olive oil in a 12-inch skillet and place over medium-high heat. When the garlic has lightly browned on all sides, remove it and add the tomatoes to the pan. Season with salt and cook until most of the liquid they release has evaporated, 6 to 8 minutes.
5. While the tomatoes are cooking, remove the peppers from the plastic bag and remove the skin, core, and seeds. Don't rinse them or you'll wash away the flavor. Cut the peppers into narrow strips ¼ inch wide and 1 to 1½ inches long.
6. When the tomatoes are ready, add about 2 tablespoons salt to the boiling pasta water, add the fusilli, and stir well. Cook until al dente.
7. After putting the pasta in, add the roasted pepper strips to the sauce, lower the heat to medium, and season with pepper and lightly with salt. Finely chop enough parsley to measure about 1 tablespoon. Add it to the sauce along with the capers and continue cooking until the pasta is ready. When the pasta is done, drain well, toss with the sauce and the Pecorino Romano cheese, and serve at once.

FUSILLI *with* ZUCCHINI *and* MINT

 Fusilli alle Zucchine e Mentuccia

Zucchini and mint seem ideally suited to each other. One of my students' favorite vegetable dishes is a sautéed zucchini-and-mint recipe from my book, *Every Night Italian*. The important thing here is to cut the zucchini into narrow enough strips and sauté them long enough to develop a rich, sweet flavor.

SERVES 4

1. Fill a pot for the pasta with about 6 quarts of water, place over high heat, and bring to a boil.

2. Peel and thinly slice the onion crosswise. Put the olive oil in a 12-inch skillet, add the sliced onion, and place over medium-high heat. Season lightly with salt and sauté until the onion turns a rich golden color, 6 to 8 minutes.

3. While the onion is sautéing, peel and finely chop the garlic. Finely chop enough parsley to measure 2 tablespoons. Wash the zucchini, trim the ends, and cut into narrow strips ¼ inch wide and 1 to 1½ inches long. To get narrow strips you will need to cut the zucchini lengthwise into ¼-inch-thick slices.

4. When the onion is ready, add the garlic and parsley. Stir for 10 to 15 seconds, then add the zucchini. Season with salt and cook, stirring occasionally, until the zucchini is very tender and lightly browned in places, about 10 minutes.

5. After the zucchini has cooked for 5 minutes, add about 2 tablespoons salt to the boiling pasta water, add the fusilli, and stir well. Cook until al dente.

6. While the zucchini is cooking, chop the mint medium-fine and coarsely chop the basil. After the zucchini has cooked 8 minutes, add the mint and basil. When the zucchini is ready, remove from the heat.

7. Just before the pasta is done, put the skillet with the zucchini back over high heat and add 2 to 3 tablespoons of the pasta water. Stir to loosen and dissolve all the browned bits on the bottom of the skillet, then remove from the heat.

8. When the pasta is done, drain well, toss with the sauce, and serve at once.

½ medium to large sweet yellow onion

4 tablespoons extra-virgin olive oil

Salt

1 medium clove garlic

6–7 sprigs flat-leaf Italian parsley

1¼ pounds small zucchini

1 pound fusilli

1 sprig fresh mint

8–10 fresh basil leaves

LINGUINE *with* ZUCCHINI *and* ONIONS

Linguine alle Zucchine e Cipolle

My mother used to teach a dish of zucchini sautéed with sliced onions that was always a favorite of the students at her cooking school in Bologna. This is a variation that I find is delicious as a pasta sauce. Do not be afraid of overcooking the zucchini. This is a sauce, after all, and cooking the zucchini longer makes them richer and sweeter.

SERVES 4

1 medium to large sweet
yellow onion

4 tablespoons butter

Salt

1¼ pounds zucchini

Freshly ground black pepper

1 pound linguine

⅓ cup freshly grated
Parmigiano-Reggiano

1. Fill a pot for the pasta with about 6 quarts of water, place over high heat, and bring to a boil.

2. Peel the onions and very thinly slice them crosswise. Put the butter in a 12-inch skillet, add the sliced onions, and place over medium-high heat. Season lightly with salt and sauté until the onions begin to turn a rich, golden color, 6 to 8 minutes.

3. While the onions are sautéing, wash the zucchini, cut off the ends, and slice into half moons about ⅛ inch thick.

4. When the onions are ready, add the zucchini and season with salt and pepper. Cook, stirring occasionally, until the zucchini are quite tender and have started lightly browning, 12 to 15 minutes.

5. After the zucchini have cooked about 10 minutes, add about 2 tablespoons salt to the boiling pasta water, add the linguine, and stir until all the strands are submerged. Cook until al dente.

6. When the pasta is done, drain well, toss with the sauce and the Parmigiano-Reggiano, and serve at once.

Fettuccine *with* Zucchini *in a* Saffron Cream Sauce

Fettuccine alle Zucchine e Zafferano

Saffron has the distinction of being the world's most expensive spice by weight. It is actually the red stamens of a purple crocus flower, and it takes about 5,000 flowers to produce an ounce of saffron. Thankfully, the amount needed in the average recipe is so small that it is affordable to use. In this elegant sauce the cream takes on the flavor of the saffron and the zucchini. It is perfectly suited to the delicate flavor and texture of egg pasta.

SERVES 4

¾ cup heavy cream

About 20 saffron strands

½ large sweet yellow onion

3 tablespoons butter

1¼ pound zucchini

Salt

Freshly ground black pepper

10 ounces dried egg fettuccine

⅓ cup freshly grated Parmigiano-Reggiano

1. Put the heavy cream in a small saucepan. Crumble the saffron strands between your fingers into the pan. Cover and place over low heat.
2. Fill a pot for the pasta with about 6 quarts of water, place over high heat, and bring to a boil.
3. Peel the onion and finely chop it. Put the butter in a 12-inch skillet, add the chopped onion, and place over medium-high heat. Sauté until the onion turns a rich golden color, about 5 minutes.
4. While the onion is sautéing, cut the zucchini into narrow, ⅛-inch-thick sticks 1 to 1½ inches long. To accomplish this it will be necessary to cut the zucchini lengthwise into ⅛-inch-thick slices first. When the onion is ready, add the zucchini, season with salt and pepper, and continue cooking until the zucchini is tender and lightly browned, 10 to 12 minutes. Add the hot cream and saffron that is in the saucepan and continue cooking until the sauce thickens a little and the cream is reduced by about one-third, 1 to 2 minutes, then remove from the heat.
5. While the cream is reducing, add about 2 tablespoons salt to the boiling pasta water, add the fettuccine, and stir until all the strands are submerged. Cook until al dente.
6. When the pasta is done, drain well, toss with the sauce and the Parmigiano-Reggiano, and serve at once.

FUSILLI *with* YELLOW SQUASH *and* GRAPE TOMATOES

 Fusilli con le Zucchine Gialle e Ciliegini

This is a dish that was originally inspired by my then-five-year-old daughter, Gabriella. While we were shopping together at our local supermarket, she picked up a package of yellow squash and one of grape tomatoes and asked me, "Can we cook these together tonight?" So we took them home and I sautéed the squash "Italian style" in olive oil with some sliced onion and herbs, adding the grape tomatoes toward the end. It became a favorite vegetable side dish in our family, and I decided to adapt it as a pasta sauce.

SERVES 4

1. Fill a pot for the pasta with about 6 quarts of water, place over high heat, and bring to a boil.

2. Peel the onion, cut in half, and thinly slice lengthwise. Put the olive oil in a 12-inch skillet, add the sliced onion, and place over medium–high heat. Sauté until the onion begins to lightly brown, 6 to 8 minutes.

3. While the onion is sautéing, chop enough thyme to measure 1 teaspoon and add it to the onions. Wash the yellow squash and cut off the ends. If it is the crookneck variety, cut the neck into ¼-inch half rounds and the wider part into ¼-inch quarter rounds. If it is the kind that has the same shape as a zucchini, cut all of it into ¼-inch quarter rounds.

4. When the onion is ready, add the yellow squash and season with salt and pepper. Continue cooking over medium–high heat until the squash begins to brown and is mostly tender, about 10 minutes.

5. While the squash is cooking, rinse the grape tomatoes and cut them in half lengthwise. When the squash is ready, add the tomatoes and continue cooking until they begin to break down, 6 to 8 minutes.

6. As soon as the tomatoes are in the pan, and the water for the pasta is boiling, add about 2 tablespoons salt to the boiling water, add the fusilli, and stir well. Cook until al dente.

7. When the pasta is done, toss it with the sauce and serve at once.

1 large sweet yellow onion

4 tablespoons extra-virgin olive oil

2 sprigs fresh thyme

1¼ pounds yellow squash

Salt

Freshly ground black pepper

8 ounces grape or cherry tomatoes (about 1 cup)

1 pound fusilli

PENNE *with* SPINACH *and* RICOTTA

 Penne agli Spinaci e Ricotta

When making tortelloni filled with spinach and ricotta, I sometimes ended up with leftover filling. It occurred to me that it would make a very nice pasta sauce, so I added a little cream to the mixture and it was delicious—so much so that I've been making it just to use as a pasta sauce. If you use packaged baby spinach, it is also very quick and simple to prepare.

SERVES 4

1. Fill a pot for the pasta with about 6 quarts of water, place over high heat, and bring to a boil.

2. Put about 1 inch of water in a pot large enough to cook the spinach. Place it over high heat. When the water boils, add 1 teaspoon salt and the spinach. Cook until the spinach is quite tender, 5 to 6 minutes. Drain in a colander and squeeze out as much water as possible by pressing on the spinach with a spoon. Transfer the spinach to a cutting board and finely chop it.

3. While the spinach is cooking, peel the onion and finely chop it. Put the butter in a 12-inch skillet, add the onion, and place over medium-high heat. Sauté the onion until it turns a rich golden color, about 5 minutes.

4. When the water for the pasta is boiling, add about 2 tablespoons salt, add the penne, and stir well. Cook until al dente.

5. When the onion is ready, add the spinach and sauté, stirring often, for about 5 minutes. Add the ricotta, cream, and nutmeg, and cook until the ricotta has heated through and the cream is reduced, 2 to 3 minutes. Taste and adjust for salt and season with pepper, then remove from the heat.

6. When the pasta is done, drain well, toss with the sauce and the Parmigiano-Reggiano, and serve at once.

Salt

6 ounces fresh baby spinach

½ medium yellow onion

2 tablespoons butter

1 pound penne

¾ cup whole-milk ricotta

⅓ cup heavy cream

⅛ teaspoon freshly grated whole nutmeg

Freshly ground black pepper

½ cup freshly grated Parmigiano-Reggiano

PENNE *with an* HERB-FLAVORED PINK SAUCE

Penne con la Panna Rosa e Erbe Aromatiche

Cream sauces need not be heavy and cloying. One of cream's attributes is that it is a marvelous carrier of flavors. In this sauce a relatively modest amount of cream is able to envelop your palate with the fragrant aromas of fresh herbs. I like using a beef bouillon cube for a richer flavor, but you could substitute a vegetable bouillon cube to make this a completely vegetarian dish.

SERVES 4

1½ pounds fresh tomatoes

12 fresh basil leaves

1 sprig fresh rosemary

1 sprig fresh sage

3 tablespoons butter

½ large beef or vegetable bouillon cube

Salt

1 pound penne

½ cup heavy cream

1. Fill a pot for the pasta with about 6 quarts of water, place over high heat, and bring to a boil.
2. Peel the tomatoes and coarsely chop. Finely chop half the basil leaves and enough of the rosemary and sage to measure 1 teaspoon each.
3. Put the butter and half bouillon cube in a 10-inch skillet and place over medium-high heat. Break up the bouillon cube with a wooden spoon. When it has completely dissolved and the butter has melted, add the chopped herbs. Sauté the herbs for about 1 minute, then add the tomatoes. Season with salt and cook until the tomatoes have reduced and are no longer watery, 8 to 10 minutes.
4. Add about 2 tablespoons salt to the boiling pasta water, add the penne, and stir well. Cook until al dente.
5. When the tomatoes are ready, add the heavy cream to the sauce. Finely shred the remaining basil leaves and add them to the pan. Cook until the cream has reduced by about one-third, 2 to 3 minutes, then remove from the heat.
6. When the pasta is done, drain it well and toss with the sauce. Serve at once.

PENNE *with* FOUR CHEESES

 Penne ai Quattro Formaggi

Pasta with cheese has a universal appeal and here the pleasure is increased fourfold. I particularly like how these cheeses balance each other. The pronounced flavor of gorgonzola, the richness of fontina, the savoriness of Parmigiano-Reggiano, and the delicate creaminess of mascarpone complement each other perfectly. Use the creamy gorgonzola dolce, not the dry, aged kind.

SERVES 4

1. Fill a pot for the pasta with about 6 quarts of water, place over high heat, and bring to a boil.
2. Cut the fontina into small dice.
3. When the water for the pasta is boiling, add about 2 tablespoons salt, add the penne, and stir well. Cook until al dente.
4. While the pasta is cooking, put the butter and heavy cream in a 10-inch skillet or shallow saucepan and place over medium heat. When the butter has melted, add the fontina, gorgonzola, and mascarpone. Season with salt and cook, stirring almost constantly, until all the cheeses have melted and you obtain a smooth mixture. Lower the heat to its lowest setting.
5. When the pasta is done, drain well, toss with the sauce and the Parmigiano-Reggiano, and serve at once.

4 ounces fontina

Salt

1 pound penne (maccheroni or rigatoni are also good)

1 tablespoon butter

½ cup heavy cream

2 ounces gorgonzola

2 ounces mascarpone

⅓ cup freshly grated Parmigiano-Reggiano

Spaghetti *with* Carrots

Spaghetti alle Carote

The humble carrot is really quite versatile and flavorful. You can make a cake with it, serve it as a side vegetable, or make a rich and sweet pasta sauce. To give the pasta even more carrot flavor, I cook it in the water I boiled the carrots in. This dish is great paired with a nice cold beer.

SERVES 4

1 pound carrots

Salt

6–7 sprigs flat-leaf Italian parsley

4 tablespoons butter

Freshly ground black pepper

1 pound spaghetti

¼ cup heavy cream

¼ teaspoon freshly grated nutmeg

⅓ cup freshly grated Parmigiano-Reggiano

1. Fill a pot for the pasta with about 6 quarts of water, place over high heat, and bring to a boil.
2. Trim the ends of the carrots and peel them.
3. When the water is boiling, add about 2 tablespoons salt, add the carrots, and cook until tender, 10 to 12 minutes.
4. While the carrots are cooking, finely chop enough parsley to measure about 2 tablespoons.
5. When the carrots are tender, pull them out of the boiling water (don't discard the water, and keep the pot over the heat). Very finely chop the carrots in a food processor. Put the butter in a 12-inch skillet and place over medium-high heat. When the butter has melted, add the chopped carrots. Season generously with salt and pepper and sauté, stirring often, for 4 to 5 minutes.
6. While the carrots are sautéing, add the spaghetti to the pot with the boiling water, stir until all the strands are submerged, and cook until al dente.
7. After the carrots have finished sautéing, add the heavy cream, nutmeg, and parsley. Stir for about 1 minute and remove from the heat.
8. When the pasta is done, drain well, toss with the sauce and the Parmigiano-Reggiano, and serve at once.

Penne *with* Mushrooms *and* Fresh Tomatoes

Penne alla Boscaiola

Boscaiola means "woodsman style," and this is the classic sauce that one would make after a successful mushroom-hunting expedition. Dried porcini are used here to give the cultivated mushrooms some of the depth and flavor of wild mushrooms. Cremini are marginally better than white mushrooms, though both are fine. If you can get fresh shiitake mushrooms, you can also use a combination of white or cremini and shiitake mushrooms.

SERVES 4

1 ounce dried porcini mushrooms

½ medium yellow onion

3 tablespoons extra-virgin olive oil

¾ pound fresh cremini or white mushrooms

Salt

1 pound fresh tomatoes

Freshly ground black pepper

6–7 sprigs flat-leaf Italian parsley

1 pound penne (shells are also good here)

1. Put the dried porcini in a bowl, add enough warm water to cover, and soak for at least 10 minutes.
2. Fill a pot for the pasta with about 6 quarts of water, place over high heat, and bring to a boil.
3. Peel the onion and finely chop it. Put it with olive oil in a 12-inch skillet and place over medium-high heat. Sauté until the onion turns a rich golden color, about 5 minutes. While the onion is sautéing, brush away any dirt from the fresh mushrooms and thinly slice them.
4. When the onion is done, lift the porcini out of the water, squeezing the excess back into the bowl. Do not discard the water. Coarsely chop the porcini and add them to the pan. Season lightly with salt and stir well. Strain the porcini water through a paper towel and add to the pan. Raise the heat to high and cook until the liquid has evaporated almost completely.
5. While the porcini water is reducing, peel the tomatoes and coarsely chop them. When the liquid in the pan has reduced, lower the heat to medium-high, add the fresh mushrooms, season with salt and pepper, and cook until the liquid released has almost completely evaporated, about 5 minutes.
6. While the mushrooms are cooking, finely chop enough parsley to measure 2 tablespoons.
7. When the mushrooms are done, reduce the heat to medium, add the tomatoes and the parsley, and season lightly with salt. Cook until the liquid released has reduced, about 5 minutes, then remove from the heat.
8. Once the tomatoes are in the pan, add about 2 tablespoons salt to the boiling pasta water, add the penne, and stir well. Cook until al dente.
9. When the pasta is done, drain well, toss with the sauce, and serve at once.

FUSILLI *with* TOMATO *and* MOZZARELLA

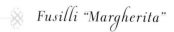
Fusilli "Margherita"

This pasta dish resembles a pizza Margherita, the basic pizza found on pizzeria menus all over Italy. Because the tomatoes are only very quickly sautéed in olive oil, I remove the seeds so the sauce will not be too watery. Make sure to drain the pasta when it is still a little underdone so that it can sit in a covered bowl to melt the mozzarella without becoming overcooked.

SERVES 4

1. Fill a pot for the pasta with about 6 quarts of water, place over high heat, and bring to a boil.

2. Peel the tomatoes and remove the seeds. Cut the flesh into ¹⁄₂-inch dice. Put the olive oil in a 12-inch skillet and place over high heat. When the oil is hot, add the tomatoes. Sauté for just 2 to 3 minutes, then season with salt and remove from the heat. Transfer to the bowl you will be serving the pasta in.

3. When the water for the pasta is boiling, add about 2 tablespoons salt, add the fusilli, and stir well. Cook until very al dente (about 30 seconds less than you normally would).

4. Coarsely chop enough oregano leaves to measure about 2 teaspoons and add them to the tomatoes in the bowl. Cut the mozzarella into small ¹⁄₄-inch dice.

5. When the pasta is done, drain well and toss with the sauce in the bowl. Add the mozzarella, toss again, then cover the bowl and let stand for about 30 seconds to allow the cheese to melt a bit. Uncover the bowl, toss one last time, and serve at once.

2 pounds fresh tomatoes

3 tablespoons extra-virgin olive oil

Salt

1 pound fusilli

2–3 sprigs fresh oregano

8 ounces fresh whole-milk mozzarella

LINGUINE *with* FRESH TOMATOES, BASIL, *and* MOZZARELLA

Linguine alla Sorrentina

Sorrento is a beautiful town on the Amalfi coast outside of Naples, an area famous for buffalo mozzarella and the sweet, flavorful tomatoes that grow there. As you drive along, you often see roadside stands offering delicious sandwiches made with mozzarella, tomatoes, and basil and drizzled with some extra-virgin olive oil. The same ingredients are used to make this classic pasta dish.

SERVES 4

1. Fill a pot for the pasta with about 6 quarts of water, place over high heat, and bring to a boil.
2. Peel, halve, and thinly slice the onion crosswise. Put the olive oil in a 12-inch skillet, add the sliced onion, and place over medium heat. Season lightly with salt and sauté until the onion becomes translucent and lightly browned, 6 to 8 minutes.
3. While the onion is sautéing, peel the tomatoes and coarsely chop them. When the onion is ready, add the tomatoes and season with salt and pepper. Cook for 5 minutes, then shred the basil and add to the tomatoes. Cook until the tomatoes have reduced and are no longer watery, 6 to 8 minutes more.
4. Add about 2 tablespoons salt to the boiling pasta water, add the linguine, and stir until all the strands are submerged. Cook until the pasta is just a bit firmer than al dente (about 30 seconds less than you normally would).
5. While the pasta and tomatoes are cooking, cut the mozzarella into small ¼-inch dice.
6. When the pasta is done, drain well and toss with the tomato sauce. Add the diced mozzarella, toss again, and cover the bowl for about 30 seconds to allow the cheese to melt. Uncover and serve at once.

1 medium yellow onion

3 tablespoons extra-virgin olive oil

Salt

2 pounds fresh tomatoes

Freshly ground black pepper

1 pound linguine (or spaghetti)

8 ounces fresh buffalo-milk mozzarella (if unavailable, use fresh, whole cow's-milk mozzarella)

10–12 fresh basil leaves

Spaghetti *with a* Meatless Carbonara

Spaghetti alle Uova

Just like in the classic carbonara sauce, raw eggs become a creamy sauce here when tossed with hot pasta. In this version there is no pancetta, only cheese and parsley, giving it a simpler, milder flavor.

SERVES 4

4 eggs

6–7 sprigs flat-leaf Italian parsley

1¼ cup freshly grated Parmigiano-Reggiano

Salt

Freshly ground black pepper

1 pound spaghetti

2 tablespoons butter

1. Fill a pot for the pasta with about 6 quarts of water, place over high heat, and bring to a boil.

2. Put 2 whole eggs and 2 yolks in the bowl you will serve the pasta in. Whisk them until the yolks and the whites are thoroughly mixed together.

3. Finely chop enough parsley to measure about 2 tablespoons and add it to the eggs. Add 1 cup of the Parmigiano-Reggiano, 1 teaspoon salt, and some grindings of black pepper. Mix well.

4. When the water for the pasta is boiling, add about 2 tablespoons salt, add the spaghetti, and stir until all the strands are submerged. Cook until al dente.

5. While the pasta is cooking, put the butter in a small saucepan over low heat. When it is melted, remove from the heat.

6. When the pasta is done, drain well and transfer to the serving bowl. Add the melted butter and mix vigorously until the pasta is well coated with the egg mixture. Serve with the remaining grated cheese sprinkled on top of each serving.

SHELLS *with* BUTTER *and* CHEESE

Conchiglie al Burro e Parmigiano

This is probably my daughter Michela's favorite pasta. The ingredients are few and so are the steps, but when it is done well, I confess this is still one my favorites, too. Though Michela prefers it plain, I find a few grindings of black pepper enhance it nicely. Other excellent pasta choices are rigatoni or maccheroni, and occasionally I also enjoy it with spaghetti.

SERVES 4

4 tablespoons butter

¼ cup heavy cream

Salt

Freshly ground black pepper

1 pound medium-sized shells

1 cup freshly grated Parmigiano-Reggiano

1. Fill a pot for the pasta with about 6 quarts of water, place over high heat, and bring to a boil.
2. Cut the butter into 6 to 8 pieces and put it in the bowl you will be serving the pasta in. Add the heavy cream and season generously with salt and pepper.
3. When the water for the pasta is boiling, add about 2 tablespoons salt, add the shells, and stir well. Cook until al dente.
4. When the pasta is done, drain well, transfer to the bowl, and mix well. Add the grated Parmigiano-Reggiano, mix again vigorously, and serve at once.

SEAFOOD
Pastas

Spaghetti *with* Shrimp, Tomatoes, *and* Capers

Spaghetti ai Gamberi, Pomodoro e Capperi

Here is a wonderfully tasty and easy shrimp pasta dish. The most time-consuming part is peeling and deveining the shrimp. Though medium shrimp are fine to use here and less expensive, I prefer using the larger 21–30 or even 16–20 per pound shrimp simply because there are fewer of them to clean that way.

SERVES 4

1 medium yellow onion

3 tablespoons extra-virgin olive oil

Salt

1 pound fresh tomatoes

¾ pound large shrimp
(see note above)

2 sprigs fresh oregano

1 tablespoon plus 1 teaspoon capers

Freshly ground black pepper

1. Fill a pot for the pasta with about 6 quarts of water, place over high heat, and bring to a boil.

2. Peel, halve, and thinly slice the onion crosswise. Put the olive oil in a 12-inch skillet, add the sliced onion, and place over medium-high heat. Season lightly with salt and sauté until the onion turns a rich golden color, 6 to 8 minutes.

3. While the onion is sautéing, peel and coarsely chop the tomatoes. When the onion is ready, add the tomatoes, season with salt, and cook until the liquid the tomatoes release has evaporated, 8 to 10 minutes.

4. While the tomatoes are cooking, peel, devein, and cut the shrimp into ½-inch pieces. Chop enough oregano to measure 2 teaspoons.

5. When the tomatoes are almost ready, add about 2 tablespoons salt to the boiling pasta water, add the spaghetti, and stir until all the strands are submerged. Cook until al dente.

6. When the tomatoes are ready, and while the pasta is cooking, add the oregano, capers, and shrimp to the pan of tomatoes. Season the shrimp with salt and pepper and cook until the shrimp turn pink through and through, about 2 minutes, then remove from the heat.

7. When the pasta is done, drain well, toss with the sauce, and serve at once.

LINGUINE *with* SHRIMP *and* PORCINI

Linguine ai Gamberi e Funghi

I love the flavor of porcini together with shrimp. Dried porcini are used here to endow the cultivated mushrooms with some porcini flavor. I use this technique often in the States, where fresh porcini are hard to get, if not prohibitively expensive.

SERVES 4

1. Put the dried porcini in a bowl, cover with warm water and soak for 10 minutes.

2. Fill a pot for the pasta with about 6 quarts of water, place over high heat, and bring to a boil.

3. Peel and finely slice the onion lengthwise. Put the olive oil in a 12-inch skillet, add the sliced onion, and place over medium–high heat. Sauté until the onion turns a rich golden color, 4 to 6 minutes. While the onion is sautéing, brush any dirt off the fresh mushrooms, then thinly slice them.

4. When the onion is ready, lift the porcini out of the water, squeezing the excess back into the bowl. Do not discard the porcini water. Coarsely chop the porcini, add them to the pan, and season lightly with salt. Strain the porcini water through a paper towel and add to the pan. Raise the heat to high and cook until almost all the liquid has evaporated.

5. While the liquid in the pan is evaporating, peel the tomatoes and coarsely chop them. Peel the shrimp, deveining if necessary, and cut into 1/2-inch pieces.

6. When most of the liquid in the pan has evaporated, lower the heat to medium–high, add the fresh mushrooms, and season with salt and pepper. Cook until the liquid the mushrooms release has evaporated completely.

7. Add about 2 tablespoons salt to the boiling pasta water, add the linguine, and stir until all the strands are submerged. Cook until al dente.

8. Add the tomatoes to the pan with the mushrooms, season lightly with salt, and cook until the liquid the tomatoes release has evaporated, 2 to 3 minutes. Add the heavy cream and the shrimp. When the cream has reduced by about one-third, and the shrimp have turned pink, 1 to 2 minutes, remove the pan from the heat.

9. When the pasta is done, drain well, toss with the sauce, and serve at once.

1 ounce dried porcini mushrooms

1/2 medium yellow onion

3 tablespoons extra-virgin olive oil

1/2 pound white or cremini mushrooms

Salt

1/2 pound fresh tomatoes

3/4 pound large shrimp

Freshly ground black pepper

1 pound linguine

1/2 cup heavy cream

LINGUINE *with a* PINK SHRIMP SAUCE

Linguine ai Gamberi con Panna Rosa

This is a very elegant sauce that is traditionally served with seafood-filled ravioli. A portion of the shrimp are chopped very fine, giving the sauce a consistency similar to meat sauce. Parsley at the end adds lightness and fragrance.

SERVES 4

¾ pound large shrimp

2 medium cloves garlic

2 tablespoons extra-virgin olive oil

2 tablespoons tomato paste

½ cup dry white wine

Salt

Freshly ground black pepper

1 pound linguine

6–7 sprigs flat-leaf Italian parsley

1 cup heavy cream

1. Fill a pot for the pasta with about 6 quarts of water, place over high heat, and bring to a boil.

2. Peel and devein the shrimp. Cut one-third of the shrimp into ½-inch pieces and leave the rest whole.

3. Peel and lightly crush the garlic cloves. Put the olive oil in a 12-inch skillet, add the garlic, and place over medium-high heat. Sauté until the garlic cloves are lightly browned on all sides, then remove them and discard.

4. While the garlic is sautéing, dissolve the tomato paste in the white wine. After removing the garlic cloves, add the wine with dissolved tomato paste to the pan and cook until the liquid has reduced by about half.

5. Add the whole shrimp and season with salt and pepper. Cook until the shrimp have turned pink, 2 to 3 minutes, then remove the pan from the heat.

6. When the water for the pasta is boiling, add about 2 tablespoons salt, add the linguine, and stir until all the strands are submerged. Cook until al dente.

7. Finely chop enough parsley to measure 2 tablespoons. Use a slotted spoon to transfer the cooked shrimp to a food processor. Pulse until the shrimp are chopped to a medium-fine consistency, then return them to the pan. Place the pan back over medium-high heat and add the cream. Cook until the cream has reduced by about half, then add the raw shrimp and the parsley. Season lightly with salt and cook until the shrimp pieces turn pink, 1 to 2 minutes, then remove the pan from the heat.

8. When the pasta is done, drain well, toss with the sauce, and serve at once.

SPAGHETTI *with* SCALLOPS

Spaghetti alle Cappe Sante

This simple, tasty scallop sauce is one I learned from my mother. It's really just scallops sautéed with garlic and parsley, but what makes it special are the breadcrumbs, which soak up the scallop flavor and cling to the pasta. My mother always used bay scallops, but it's easier to find good sea scallops and I've discovered I prefer them here.

SERVES 4

1 pound sea scallops

2 medium cloves garlic

6–7 sprigs flat-leaf Italian parsley

Salt

1 pound spaghetti (spaghettini is also good)

¼ teaspoon hot red pepper flakes

6 tablespoons extra-virgin olive oil

2 tablespoons breadcrumbs

1. Fill a pot for the pasta with about 6 quarts of water, place over high heat, and bring to a boil.

2. Cut three-quarters of the scallops into ½-inch dice. Finely chop the remaining scallops.

3. Peel and finely chop the garlic. Finely chop enough parsley to measure about 2 tablespoons.

4. When the water for the pasta is boiling, add about 2 tablespoons salt, add the spaghetti, and stir until all the strands are submerged. Cook until al dente.

5. Put the garlic, parsley, hot red pepper flakes, and 4 tablespoons of the olive oil in a 12-inch skillet and place over medium-high heat. When the garlic is sizzling, add the diced scallops. Raise the heat to high, season with salt, and cook until they have lost their translucent color, 2 to 3 minutes. Add the chopped scallops; season them with salt and cook, stirring, for another minute. The bottom of the pan at this point should have some browned cooking residue. Add a couple of tablespoons of the pasta water to loosen those tasty bits from the bottom of the pan, then remove from the heat. (If there is no browning at the bottom of the pan, don't worry about it and don't add any pasta water).

6. When the pasta is done, drain well and toss with the scallops. Add the remaining 2 tablespoons olive oil and the breadcrumbs, toss again, and serve at once.

LINGUINE *with* FISH RAGÙ

Linguine al Ragù di Pesce

Though the word *ragù* usually implies a meat sauce, here it refers to a sauce made with fish. Unlike a meat ragù, which needs to cook for a long time, a fish ragù is quick to prepare. Any firm-fleshed fish that is not too oily will work well here.

SERVES 4

1. Fill a pot for the pasta with about 6 quarts of water, place over high heat, and bring to a boil.
2. Peel and finely chop the onion. Put 3 tablespoons of the olive oil and the hot red pepper flakes in a 12-inch skillet, add the chopped onion, and place over medium–high heat. Sauté the onion until it turns a rich golden color, about 5 minutes.
3. While the onion is sautéing, peel and finely chop the garlic. Peel and coarsely chop the tomatoes.
4. When the onion is ready, add the garlic and sauté for about 30 seconds, then add the tomatoes. Season with salt and cook until the liquid the tomatoes release has evaporated, 10 to 12 minutes.
5. While the tomatoes are cooking, finely chop enough parsley to measure about 2 tablespoons. Cut the fish into strips about ½ inch thick and 1 inch long.
6. When the tomatoes are almost ready, add about 2 tablespoons salt to the boiling pasta water, add the linguine, and stir until all the strands are submerged. Cook until al dente.
7. While the pasta is cooking, add the fish and the parsley to the tomatoes. Season the fish with salt and cook until it is cooked through, 2 to 3 minutes. Remove the pan from the heat.
8. When the pasta is done, drain well, toss with the sauce and the remaining tablespoon of olive oil, and serve at once.

½ medium yellow onion

4 tablespoons extra-virgin olive oil

⅛ teaspoon hot red pepper flakes

1 medium clove garlic

1½ pounds fresh tomatoes

Salt

6–7 sprigs flat-leaf Italian parsley

8 ounces Atlantic snapper fillet (grouper, halibut, and striped bass are also excellent)

1 pound linguine

LINGUINE *with* CRAB *and* ARUGULA

 Linguine al Granchio e Rucola

I first had a version of this delicious pasta dish in Positano, on the beautiful Amalfi coast. The flavors of sweet crab meat, spicy arugula, and fresh tomatoes balance each other perfectly. Dungeness crab is ideal, if you can get it; otherwise use any good, sweet-tasting, meaty crab.

SERVES 4

1. Fill a pot for the pasta with about 6 quarts of water, place over high heat, and bring to a boil.

2. Peel and finely chop the garlic. Peel the tomatoes, remove the seeds, and cut into ¼-inch dice.

3. Put the olive oil, garlic, and hot red pepper flakes in a 12-inch skillet and place over medium-high heat. Once the garlic is sizzling, add the tomatoes, season with salt, and raise the heat to high. Cook quickly, for 2 to 3 minutes, just until the tomatoes begin to break down but not to the point of becoming a sauce. Stir often to prevent the tomatoes from sticking to the bottom of the pan.

4. While the tomatoes are cooking, wash the arugula, remove any thick stems, then coarsely chop it.

5. When the water for the pasta is boiling, add about 2 tablespoons salt, add the linguine, and stir until all the strands are submerged. Cook until al dente.

6. When the tomatoes are ready, add the chopped arugula and season with salt. Reduce the heat to medium-high and cook until the arugula has completely wilted, 2 to 3 minutes. Add the crab and continue cooking, stirring well, until it has heated through, 1 to 2 minutes.

7. When the pasta is done, drain well, toss with the sauce, and serve at once.

1 medium clove garlic

1¼ pounds fresh tomatoes

5 tablespoons extra-virgin olive oil

¼ teaspoon hot red pepper flakes

Salt

2 ounces arugula

1 pound linguine

8 ounces cooked lump crab meat

Linguine *with* Clams *and* Zucchini

Linguine alle Vongole e Zucchine

The combination of clams and zucchini is typical in Naples and the surrounding area. The sweet flavor of zucchini with peppery, savory clams is a match made in heaven. Just like in the classic clam sauce, the pasta finishes cooking in the liquid the clams release, imbuing it with clam flavor. The most flavorful and tender clams are littleneck or similar small clams such as manila clams, Cedar Key, Florida clams, or mahogany clams from Maine.

SERVES 4

½ large yellow onion

4 tablespoons extra-virgin olive oil

1 medium clove garlic

1 pound zucchini

Salt

Freshly ground black pepper

2–3 dozen littleneck clams, depending on size

⅓ cup dry white wine

1 pound linguine (spaghetti is also good)

12–14 fresh basil leaves

1. Fill a pot for the pasta with about 6 quarts of water, place over high heat, and bring to a boil.

2. Peel and finely chop the onion. Put the olive oil in a deep, wide skillet large enough to accommodate the pasta later, add the chopped onion, and place over medium–high heat. Sauté until the onion turns a rich golden color, about 5 minutes.

3. While the onion is sautéing, peel and finely chop the garlic. Wash the zucchini, trim the ends, and cut into ½-inch chunks.

4. When the onion is ready, add the garlic, sauté for about 30 seconds, then add the zucchini. Season with salt and pepper and sauté until the zucchini is tender and lightly browned, 10 to 12 minutes. If the zucchini releases a lot of liquid, raise the heat a bit.

5. While the zucchini is cooking, rinse the clams in several changes of cold water, but don't let them soak. Discard any clams that are open and don't close when tapped.

6. When the zucchini is ready, raise the heat to high and add the wine. Let it bubble for about 30 seconds to allow the alcohol to evaporate, then add the clams and cover the pan. Cook over medium–high heat until all the clams are open, 2 to 3 minutes (if any clams don't open, they are probably empty or full of sand, and you should discard them). Remove the pan from the heat.

7. While the clams are cooking, add about 2 tablespoons salt to the boiling pasta water, add the linguine, and stir until all the strands are submerged. Cook until very al dente, about a minute before they are done.

8. While the pasta is cooking, take out the clams, remove the meat from the shells, and return it to the pan (discard the shells). Coarsely chop the basil and stir it into the sauce.

9. When the pasta is ready, drain well, and put it in the pan with the sauce (if the pasta is done before you are finished with the clams, drain it and put in the sauce until you are ready to continue). Return the pan to medium–high heat and cook, stirring often, until the pasta has absorbed all the liquid in the pan. The pasta needs to cook another 1 to 2 minutes, so if there isn't very much liquid in the pan, cover the pan; if there is more liquid, cook uncovered. When the pasta is done, serve at once.

Linguine *with* Shrimp *and* Zucchini

Linguine ai Gamberi e Zucchine

Shrimp and zucchini is another favorite Italian shellfish-and-vegetable combination. A little tomato gives this quick and delicious sauce a light, fresh flavor that is great with linguine or spaghetti.

SERVES 4

½ medium yellow onion

3 tablespoons extra-virgin olive oil

1 medium clove garlic

¾ pound zucchini

Freshly ground black pepper

Salt

¾ pound fresh tomatoes

¾ pound large shrimp

1 pound linguine (spaghetti is also good)

1. Fill a pot for the pasta with about 6 quarts of water, place over high heat, and bring to a boil.

2. Peel the onion and finely chop it. Put the olive oil in a 12-inch skillet, add the chopped onion, and place over medium-high heat. Sauté until the onion turns a rich golden color, about 5 minutes.

3. Peel and thinly slice the garlic. Wash the zucchini, trim the ends, and cut into ½-inch chunks. When the onion is ready, add the garlic, sauté for about 30 seconds, then add the zucchini. Season with pepper and lightly with salt and continue sautéing until the zucchini begins to brown, about 5 minutes.

4. While the zucchini is sautéing, peel and coarsely chop the tomatoes. When the zucchini is ready, add the tomatoes. Season lightly with salt and lower the heat to medium. Cook until the liquid the tomatoes release has almost completely evaporated, 6 to 8 minutes.

5. While the sauce is cooking, peel and devein the shrimp. Cut them into ½-inch pieces.

6. When the tomatoes are almost done, add about 2 tablespoons salt to the boiling pasta water, add the linguine, and stir until all the strands are submerged. Cook until al dente.

7. When the tomatoes have reduced, add the shrimp to the sauce, season them with salt, and cook until they turn completely pink, 2 to 3 minutes.

8. When the pasta is done, drain well, toss with the sauce, and serve at once.

SPAGHETTI *with* SHRIMP *and* SCALLOPS

 Spaghetti ai Gamberi e Cappe Sante

In my first book, *The Classic Pasta Cookbook*, I have a recipe for a seafood lasagne with a shrimp-and-scallop filling that has always received rave reviews. I have adapted that filling as a light and tasty seafood sauce.

SERVES 4

1. Fill a pot for the pasta with about 6 quarts of water, place over high heat, and bring to a boil.
2. Peel and finely chop the onion. Put the olive oil in a 12-inch skillet, add the chopped onion, and place over medium-high heat. Sauté until the onion turns a rich golden color, about 5 minutes.
3. Peel and finely chop the garlic. Finely chop enough parsley to measure about 1½ tablespoons. Peel the shrimp, devein if necessary, and cut into ½-inch chunks. Cut the scallops into ½-inch dice.
4. When the water for the pasta is boiling, add about 2 tablespoons salt, add the spaghetti, and stir until all the strands are submerged. Cook until al dente.
5. Add the garlic and parsley to the sautéed onion and cook, stirring, for about 30 seconds. Raise the heat to high and add the wine. After the wine has almost completely evaporated, add the shrimp and scallops, season with salt and pepper, and cook, stirring often, until the shrimp have turned pink and the scallops are cooked through, 2 to 3 minutes. Add about 2 tablespoons of the pasta water, loosen all the browned bits from the bottom of the pan, then remove from the heat.
6. When the pasta is done, drain well, toss with the sauce, and serve at once.

½ medium yellow onion

4 tablespoons extra-virgin olive oil

1 medium clove garlic

5–6 sprigs flat-leaf Italian parsley

½ pound large shrimp

½ pound sea scallops

Salt

1 pound spaghetti (linguine is also good)

¼ cup dry white wine

Freshly ground black pepper

Linguine *with* Lobster *and* Asparagus

Linguine all'Astice e Asparagi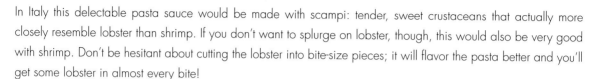

In Italy this delectable pasta sauce would be made with scampi: tender, sweet crustaceans that actually more closely resemble lobster than shrimp. If you don't want to splurge on lobster, though, this would also be very good with shrimp. Don't be hesitant about cutting the lobster into bite-size pieces; it will flavor the pasta better and you'll get some lobster in almost every bite!

SERVES 4

½ pound asparagus

Salt

½ large yellow onion

3 tablespoons extra-virgin olive oil

¾ pound fresh tomatoes

1 pound linguine

13–14 ounces Maine lobster tails

Freshly ground black pepper

1. Fill a pot for the pasta with about 6 quarts of water, place over high heat, and bring to a boil.

2. Fill a skillet with water that will accommodate the asparagus and place it over high heat. Cut off the white, woody bottom part of the asparagus spears, then peel the remaining bottom third. When the water in the skillet is boiling, add 1 teaspoon salt and gently slide in the asparagus. Cook until it is are tender, 5 to 6 minutes, then lift it out and set aside.

3. While the asparagus is cooking, peel the onion and finely chop it. Put the olive oil in a 12-inch skillet, add the chopped onion, and place over medium-high heat. Sauté until the onion turns a rich golden color, about 5 minutes.

4. When the asparagus is ready, cut into 1-inch lengths. Once the onion is ready, add the asparagus and sauté for 2 to 3 minutes.

5. While the asparagus is sautéing, peel the tomatoes and coarsely chop. When the asparagus is ready, add the tomatoes to the pan, season with salt, and cook until the liquid released has almost completely evaporated, 3 to 4 minutes.

6. While the tomatoes are cooking, add about 2 tablespoons salt to the boiling pasta water, add the linguine, and stir until all the strands are submerged. Cook until al dente.

7. While the pasta is cooking, use a sharp pair of scissors to cut the shell of the lobster tail along the back and the belly. Gently remove the lobster meat and cut it into ½-inch chunks. When the tomatoes are ready, add the lobster, season with salt and pepper, and cook until the lobster is cooked through, about 2 minutes.

8. When the pasta is done, drain well, toss with the sauce, and serve at once.

SPAGHETTI *with* MUSSELS

I use a similar technique here to the one I use when making sauces with clams, which is to finish cooking the pasta in the sauce with the juices the mussels release. That way the pasta soaks up all their flavor. In Italy pasta is often served with clams and mussels in the shell. I find American clam shells are too heavy, so I always take them out, but mussel shells are light enough to leave in, which makes for a nice presentation.

SERVES 4

1. Fill a pot for the pasta with about 6 quarts of water, place over high heat, and bring to a boil.
2. Wash the mussels in several changes of cold water and remove any beards.
3. Peel the tomatoes and coarsely chop.
4. Peel the garlic and finely chop it. Finely chop enough parsley to measure 1 tablespoon and put it with the garlic, olive oil, and hot red pepper flakes in a deep skillet large enough to hold the pasta later. Place over medium-high heat. After the garlic has sizzled for about 15 seconds, add the wine. Let it bubble for 1 to 2 minutes to evaporate the alcohol, then add the tomatoes. Season with salt and cook for about 2 minutes, then shred the basil and add it to the sauce. Continue to cook the tomatoes until they begin to break down into a sauce, about 3 minutes more.
5. Add about 2 tablespoons salt to the boiling pasta water, add the spaghetti, and stir until all the strands are submerged. Cook until very al dente, about 1 minute less than you normally would.
6. While the pasta is cooking, put the mussels in the pan with the sauce and cover. Cook until all the mussels have opened, 3 to 4 minutes (if any mussels don't open, they are probably empty or full of sand, and you should discard them). Remove from the heat.
7. When the pasta is ready, drain well, and put it in the pan with the sauce. Return the pan to medium-high heat and cook, stirring often, until the pasta has absorbed all the liquid in the pan. The pasta needs to cook another 1 to 2 minutes, so if there isn't very much liquid in the pan, cover the pan; if there is more liquid, cook uncovered. When the pasta is done, serve at once.

3 dozen mussels (about 1½ pounds)

1 pound fresh tomatoes

1 medium clove garlic

3–4 sprigs flat-leaf Italian parsley

3 tablespoons extra-virgin olive oil

⅛ teaspoon hot red pepper flakes

¼ cup dry white wine

Salt

8–10 fresh basil leaves

1 pound spaghetti

Spaghetti *with* Scallops, Fresh Tomatoes, *and* Basil

Spaghetti al Pomodoro e Cappe Sante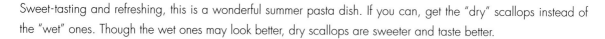

Sweet-tasting and refreshing, this is a wonderful summer pasta dish. If you can, get the "dry" scallops instead of the "wet" ones. Though the wet ones may look better, dry scallops are sweeter and taste better.

SERVES 4

1½ pounds fresh tomatoes

1 medium clove garlic

⅛ teaspoon hot red pepper flakes

3 tablespoons extra-virgin olive oil

Salt

1 pound sea scallops

1 pound spaghetti (linguine is also good)

12 fresh basil leaves

1. Fill a pot for the pasta with about 6 quarts of water, place over high heat, and bring to a boil.
2. Peel the tomatoes and coarsely chop them. Peel the garlic clove and finely chop it.
3. Put the garlic, hot red pepper flakes, and the olive oil in a 12-inch skillet and place over medium-high heat. As soon as the garlic begins to sizzle, add the tomatoes. Season with salt and cook until the liquid the tomatoes release has evaporated, 10 to 12 minutes.
4. While the tomatoes are cooking, cut the scallops into ¼-inch dice.
5. When the tomatoes are ready, add about 2 tablespoons salt to the boiling pasta water, add the spaghetti, and stir until all the strands are submerged. Cook until al dente.
6. Shred the basil leaves and add them to the pan with the tomatoes. Raise the heat to high and add the scallops. Cook until the scallops are done, 1 to 2 minutes, then remove from the heat.
7. When the pasta is done, drain well, toss with the sauce, and serve at once.

LINGUINE *with* MAHI MAHI, FRESH TOMATOES, *and* CAPERS

Linguine del Capitan

This is a dish I had at a restaurant in Verona called Al Capitan that serves fish and seafood exclusively. There is no menu; instead the young and talented chef/owner comes around to each table to explain the day's offerings. In the original version the fish used was mackerel, but in Italy mackerel is more delicate than what one usually finds in the States, so I substituted mahi mahi, which is a milder yet savory fish. Very fresh bluefish would also be a good choice.

SERVES 4

1 medium clove garlic

4–5 sprigs flat-leaf Italian parsley

1½ pounds fresh tomatoes

4 tablespoons extra-virgin olive oil

Salt

Freshly ground black pepper

¾ pound fresh mahi mahi (skinless mackerel or bluefish are also good)

1 pound linguine

2 tablespoons capers

1. Fill a pot for the pasta with about 6 quarts of water, place over high heat, and bring to a boil.
2. Peel and finely chop the garlic. Finely chop enough parsley to measure 1½ tablespoons. Peel the tomatoes and coarsely chop.
3. Put the garlic, parsley, and 3 tablespoons of the olive oil in a 12-inch skillet and place over medium-high heat. When the garlic is sizzling, add the chopped tomatoes. Season with salt and pepper and cook for about 5 minutes, until the tomatoes have mostly broken down but are still somewhat chunky.
4. While the tomatoes are cooking, cut the fish into ½-inch chunks.
5. When the water for the pasta is boiling, add about 2 tablespoons salt, add the linguine, and stir until all the strands are submerged. Cook until al dente.
6. When the tomatoes are ready, add the capers and the fish to the skillet. Season the fish with salt and pepper and cook until the fish is cooked through, 3 to 5 minutes. If there is too much liquid in the sauce, raise the heat to high and cook until the sauce has reduced.
7. When the pasta is done, drain well, toss with the sauce and the remaining tablespoon of olive oil, and serve at once.

PENNE *with* FRESH TUNA *and a* SAFFRON CREAM SAUCE

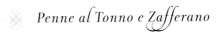

Penne al Tonno e Zafferano

Saffron and seafood go very well together and I find fresh tuna is particularly well suited to the delicate flavor of saffron. I prefer the taste of saffron in strands rather than powdered. To extract its flavor, it's necessary to let the saffron steep in the hot cream.

SERVES 4

1. Put the heavy cream in a small saucepan. Crumble the saffron strands between your fingers into the pan. Cover and place over very low heat.
2. Fill a pot for the pasta with about 6 quarts of water, place over high heat, and bring to a boil.
3. Finely chop enough parsley to measure about 1 tablespoon. Cut the tuna into ½-inch dice.
4. When the water for the pasta is boiling, add about 2 tablespoons salt, add the penne, and stir well. Cook until al dente.
5. While the pasta is cooking, peel and lightly crush the garlic and put it with the butter in a 12-inch skillet. Sauté until the garlic is lightly browned on all sides, then remove and discard. Add the tuna to the pan, season with salt and pepper, raise the heat to high, and cook until it is seared on all sides, about 2 minutes. Lower the heat to medium-high and add the hot cream and saffron and the parsley. Cook until the cream has thickened a little, 1 to 2 minutes, then remove from the heat.
6. When the pasta is done, drain well, toss with the sauce, and serve at once.

¾ cup heavy cream

About 20 saffron strands

3–4 sprigs flat-leaf Italian parsley

¾ pound fresh tuna

Salt

1 pound penne

2 medium cloves garlic

2 tablespoons butter

Freshly ground black pepper

Farfalle *with* Fresh Salmon

Farfalle al Salmone

Though salmon is not a native Italian fish and one rarely sees it on restaurant menus, its rich flavor makes for a great pasta sauce. This straightforward recipe brings out its flavor, and if salmon *were* popular in Italy, this is probably how it would be prepared.

SERVES 4

1¾ pounds fresh tomatoes

1 medium clove garlic

3 tablespoons extra-virgin olive oil

¼ teaspoon hot red pepper flakes

Salt

½ pound skinless salmon fillet

1 pound farfalle (penne or fusilli are also good)

¾ cup heavy cream

6–8 fresh basil leaves

1. Fill a pot for the pasta with about 6 quarts of water, place over high heat, and bring to a boil.
2. Peel and coarsely chop the tomatoes. Peel and finely chop the garlic. Put the olive oil in a 12-inch skillet, add the garlic and red pepper flakes, and place over medium-high heat. Sauté until the garlic is sizzling. Add the tomatoes, season with salt, and cook until all the liquid the tomatoes release has evaporated, 10 to 12 minutes.
3. While the tomatoes are cooking, cut the salmon into strips about ¼ inch thick and 1½ inch long.
4. Once the tomatoes are ready, add about 2 tablespoons salt to the boiling pasta water, add the farfalle, and stir well. Cook until al dente.
5. While the pasta is cooking, add the salmon to the pan with the tomatoes, season with salt, and add the cream. Coarsely chop the basil and add it to the pan. Cook until the cream has thickened and reduced by about one-third, 2 to 3 minutes.
6. When the pasta is done, drain well, toss with the sauce, and serve at once.

SPAGHETTI *with* OLIVES, CAPERS, *and* ANCHOVIES

Spaghetti alla Puttanesca Bianca

This is a tomato-less version of the classic Puttanesca sauce, hence the name *Bianca*, meaning "white." In the absence of tomatoes, bread crumbs are used to hold all the flavors together instead. I like using a thicker breadcrumb here; either homemade crumbs or plain panko-style store-bought breadcrumbs work well. Though you might think that very little, if any, salt is needed here, unless you season with salt at least moderately, the pasta will taste bland.

SERVES 4

1. Fill a pot for the pasta with about 6 quarts of water, place over high heat, and bring to a boil.
2. Peel and finely chop the garlic. Finely chop enough parsley to measure about 2 tablespoons. Slice the flesh of the olives away from the pits and coarsely chop.
3. When the water for the pasta is boiling, add about 2 tablespoons salt, add the spaghetti, and stir until all the strands are submerged. Cook until al dente.
4. Chop the anchovies and put them with the olive oil in an 8-inch skillet. Place over medium heat and cook until the anchovies have dissolved, about 1 minute.
5. Add the chopped garlic and sauté briefly, about 15 seconds. Add the parsley, olives, and capers and season with salt. Cook for about another minute, then remove from the heat.
6. When the pasta is done, drain well, toss with the sauce and the bread-crumbs, and serve at once.

2 medium cloves garlic

6–7 sprigs flat-leaf Italian parsley

8 Kalamata olives

Salt

1 pound spaghetti

6 anchovy fillets

6 tablespoons extra-virgin olive oil

2 tablespoons capers

2 tablespoons breadcrumbs (see note above)

BIGOLI *with* ONIONS *and* ANCHOVIES

Bigoli in Salsa

Bigoli are a specialty of the Veneto. Their shape is like thick spaghetti, but unlike spaghetti, bigoli are traditionally made by hand with a combination of soft and whole-wheat flour and water. The dough is pushed through small holes using a hand-cranked press. It is sometimes possible to find bigoli in specialty stores, but spaghetti are a perfectly good substitute. Bigoli and this anchovy-and-onion sauce is a classic pairing. Don't be alarmed by the amount of anchovies. The onion softens their flavor, and my wife, who was quite apprehensive when I first made this, was surprised by how much she liked it. This is a sauce that would also be well suited to whole-wheat pasta.

SERVES 4

1 medium sweet yellow onion

5 tablespoons extra-virgin olive oil

Freshly ground black pepper

Salt

12 anchovy fillets

4–5 sprigs flat-leaf Italian parsley

1 pound bigoli or spaghetti

1. Fill a pot for the pasta with about 6 quarts of water, place over high heat, and bring to a boil.

2. Peel, halve, and thinly slice the onion crosswise. Put it with 4 tablespoons of the olive oil in a 10-inch skillet over medium heat. Season with pepper and very lightly with salt. Sauté until the onion softens and turns a rich golden color, 6 to 8 minutes.

3. While the onion is sautéing, chop the anchovy fillets. Finely chop enough parsley to measure about 1½ tablespoons.

4. When the water for the pasta is boiling, add about 2 tablespoons salt, add the bigoli, and stir until all the strands are submerged. Cook until al dente.

5. While the pasta is cooking, put the anchovies in the pan with the onions and cook, stirring, until the anchovies dissolve. Add the parsley and 2 tablespoons of the pasta water and continue cooking for about a minute, then remove from the heat.

6. When the pasta is done, drain well, toss with the sauce and the remaining tablespoon of olive oil, and serve at once.

SPAGHETTI *with a* SAVORY TOMATO SAUCE

※ *Spaghetti alla Puttanesca*

This "saucily" sauced Neapolitan pasta dish is named after the "ladies of the night" who, according to legend, used it to seduce their clients. Though I cannot guarantee its aphrodisiac qualities, I think it will undoubtedly make whomever you serve this pasta to quite happy. My wife certainly is when I make it!

SERVES 4

1. Fill a pot for the pasta with about 6 quarts of water, place over high heat, and bring to a boil.
2. Peel the tomatoes and coarsely chop them.
3. Peel the garlic and finely chop it. Coarsely chop the anchovies and put them with the olive oil in a 12-inch skillet and place over medium-high heat. Cook until the anchovies have mostly dissolved, 1 to 2 minutes. Add the chopped garlic and let it sizzle for about 15 seconds, then add the tomatoes. Season lightly with salt and cook until most of the liquid the tomatoes release has evaporated, about 15 minutes.
4. While the tomatoes are cooking, slice the flesh of the olives away from the pits and into slivers.
5. When the tomatoes are almost done, add about 2 tablespoons salt to the boiling pasta water, add the spaghetti, and stir until all the strands are submerged. Cook until al dente.
6. When the tomatoes are ready, coarsely chop enough oregano leaves to measure about 2 teaspoons and add them to the pan along with the capers and sliced olives. Cook for about 2 minutes, then remove from the heat.
7. When the pasta is done, drain well, toss with the sauce, and serve at once.

2 pounds fresh tomatoes

1 medium clove garlic

6 anchovy fillets

4 tablespoons extra-virgin olive oil

Salt

10 Kalamata olives

1 pound spaghetti or spaghettini

2 sprigs oregano

2 tablespoons capers

Orecchiette *with* Broccoli

Orecchiette ai Broccoli

You would never guess there are anchovies in this sauce, but without them it would not have the same depth of flavor. Orecchiette, which means "little ears" in Italian, are a specialty of Apulia, where it is still possible to find women making and selling them on the street. Orecchiette are a flour-and-water pasta and you can buy them dried. The classic sauce they are paired with is made with broccoletti, a vegetable similar to broccoli rabe, and I have a recipe for it in my book *How to Cook Italian*. This version with regular broccoli is a bit milder and sweeter.

SERVES 4

1 medium clove garlic

3 anchovy fillets

Salt

1 pound broccoli florets

4 tablespoons extra-virgin olive oil

⅛ teaspoon hot red pepper flakes

1 pound orecchiette

1. Fill a pot for the pasta with about 6 quarts of water, place over high heat, and bring to a boil.
2. Fill a pot that will hold the broccoli florets with water and place over high heat.
3. Peel the garlic and finely chop it. Finely chop the anchovies.
4. When the water for the broccoli is boiling, add 1 teaspoon salt and add the broccoli. Cook until tender, 5 to 6 minutes. Drain and coarsely chop the broccoli.
5. Put the anchovies and the olive oil in a 12-inch skillet and place over medium-high heat. Once the anchovies have dissolved, add the garlic and hot red pepper flakes. After the garlic begins to sizzle, add the broccoli, season with salt, and sauté over medium heat for about 8 minutes.
6. Add about 2 tablespoons salt to the boiling pasta water, add the orecchiette, and stir well. Cook until al dente.
7. When the pasta is almost ready, stir ¼ cup of the pasta water into the broccoli. When the pasta is done, drain well, toss with the sauce, and serve at once.

SPAGHETTI *with a* SAVORY ONION SAUCE

Spaghetti alle Cipolle

Cooking is a little like alchemy. Ingredients that may not be very appealing in their raw state are transformed into something delectable. That is exactly what happens to the onions in this sauce. Even sweet onions are not something you would sit down to eat a plateful of raw, but after a relatively short cooking process, and with a few other ingredients, they become a rich, delicious sauce for pasta.

SERVES 4

2 medium sweet yellow onions

6 tablespoons extra-virgin olive oil

Salt

Freshly ground black pepper

3–4 sprigs flat-leaf Italian parsley

2 anchovy fillets

1 pound spaghetti (linguine are also good)

¼ cup dry white wine

⅓ cup freshly grated Parmigiano-Reggiano

1. Fill a pot for the pasta with about 6 quarts of water, place over high heat, and bring to a boil.
2. Peel and finely chop the onions. Put the olive oil in a 12-inch skillet, add the chopped onions, and place over medium-high heat. Season with salt and pepper and sauté until the onion turns a rich golden color, about 15 minutes.
3. While the onion is sautéing, finely chop enough parsley to measure about 1 tablespoon. Finely chop the anchovies.
4. When the onion is almost ready, add about 2 tablespoons salt to the boiling pasta water, add the spaghetti, and stir until all the strands are submerged. Cook until al dente.
5. When the onions are ready, add the white wine, parsley, and anchovies. Cook, stirring, until the wine has reduced almost completely and the anchovies have completely dissolved, about 1 minute, then remove from the heat.
6. When the pasta is done, drain well, toss with the sauce and the Parmigiano-Reggiano, and serve at once.

SPAGHETTINI *with* BLACK TRUFFLES

This dish is named after Norcia, a town in the heart of black-truffle country in Umbria. The white truffle from Alba may be the aristocrat of truffles, but the black truffle is certainly not to be scoffed at. I cannot think of a better way to eat spaghettini than enveloped in its rich, woodsy aroma and flavor. Don't be concerned about the anchovies here. You will not taste them, but they do intensify the flavor of the truffle. Use only fresh truffles, though. I have found truffles preserved in a jar to be very disappointing and not worth the expense.

SERVES 4

1. Fill a pot for the pasta with about 6 quarts of water, place over high heat, and bring to a boil.
2. Peel and lightly crush the garlic. Put the olive oil and garlic in an 8-inch skillet or saucepan over medium-high heat. Once the garlic has lightly browned on all sides, remove it and discard.
3. While the garlic is browning, finely chop the anchovies and finely grate the truffles. After removing the garlic, add the anchovies and cook, stirring, until completely dissolved, then remove from the heat.
4. When the water for the pasta is boiling, add about 2 tablespoons salt, add the spaghettini, and stir until all the strands are submerged. Cook until al dente.
5. When the pasta is almost done, return the skillet to low heat and stir in the truffles. Season lightly with salt. When the pasta is done, drain well, toss with the sauce, and serve at once.

2 medium cloves garlic

6 tablespoons extra-virgin olive oil

2 anchovy fillets

3–4 ounces fresh black truffles

Salt

1 pound spaghettini

MEAT
Pastas

Tagliatelle *with* Prosciutto

Tagliatelle alla Romagnola

Like Proust with his *madeleine*, if I close my eyes when I eat this dish I am transported to another time and place. I feel as if I were back in Cesenatico, the town on the Adriatic where my mother was born and where I spent most of my summers growing up. This is the quintessential pasta dish of the Romagna part of Emilia-Romagna: homemade egg noodles with lots of butter, prosciutto, and Parmigiano-Reggiano cheese. How can you go wrong?

SERVES 4

4 ounces prosciutto, sliced
⅛ inch thick

4 tablespoons butter

Salt

10 ounces dried egg tagliatelle

½ cup freshly grated
Parmigiano-Reggiano

1. Fill a pot for the pasta with about 6 quarts of water, place over high heat, and bring to a boil.

2. Cut the prosciutto into narrow strips about 1 inch long. Put the butter in a 10-inch skillet and place over medium heat. When the butter has melted, add the prosciutto and season lightly with salt. Cook until the prosciutto has lost its raw color but not long enough to let it brown, 1 to 2 minutes, then remove from the heat.

3. When the water for the pasta is boiling, add about 2 tablespoons salt, add the tagliatelle, and stir until all the strands are submerged. Cook until al dente.

4. When the pasta is done, drain (but not too thoroughly, so the pasta is still coated with some moisture), toss with the sauce and the grated Parmigiano-Reggiano, and serve at once.

SPAGHETTI CARBONARA

 Spaghetti alla Carbonara

The origin of this typical Roman pasta dish is as recent as the Second World War. One story, which seems more the product of a fertile imagination than fact, tells of how American soldiers would go into Roman trattorie and order bacon and eggs with a side of pasta. They were served a sunny-side-up egg and pancetta (or more likely *guanciale*, cured pork jowl) and a plate of unseasoned spaghetti. When they mixed the two, Spaghetti alla Carbonara was born. Another story says that it was invented in a small town in southern Italy called Carbonia, by a chef who later moved to Rome and named the dish after his hometown. Some people simply say it's called "Carbonara" because the generous grindings of pepper look like coal dust (*carbone* means "coal" in Italian). In any case, it is a luscious dish, whose creaminess comes from the raw eggs' contact with the hot pasta rather than cream. I like to use a combination of whole eggs and yolks, which I find makes the dish both richer and creamier.

SERVES 4

1. Fill a pot for the pasta with about 6 quarts of water, place over high heat, and bring to a boil.

2. Cut the pancetta into narrow strips about 1 inch long. Put the olive oil, butter, and pancetta in a 10-inch skillet and place over medium-high heat. Cook until the pancetta begins to brown, but not long enough to make it crisp, 2 to 3 minutes. Add the wine and cook until it has reduced by half. Remove from the heat and set aside.

3. When the water for the pasta is boiling, add about 2 tablespoons salt, add the spaghetti, and stir until all the strands are submerged. Cook until al dente.

4. While the pasta is cooking, finely chop enough parsley to measure about 1 tablespoon. Put the parsley and the grated cheeses in the bowl you'll be serving the pasta in. Add the whole eggs and yolks, and season lightly with salt and generously with pepper. Mix thoroughly.

5. When the pasta is almost ready, put the skillet with the pancetta back over medium-high heat to reheat. When the pasta is done, drain it, put it in the serving bowl, and toss it vigorously with a wooden spoon until it is well coated with the egg mixture. Pour the contents of the skillet into the bowl, toss again, and serve at once.

4 ounces pancetta, sliced ⅛ inch thick

2 tablespoons extra-virgin olive oil

2 tablespoons butter

¼ cup dry white wine

Salt

1 pound spaghetti

3–4 sprigs flat-leaf Italian parsley

¼ cup freshly grated Parmigiano-Reggiano

2 tablespoons freshly grated Pecorino Romano

2 whole eggs

2 egg yolks

Freshly ground black pepper

Spaghetti *with* Mascarpone *and* Prosciutto

Spaghetti al Mascarpone e Prosciutto

Mascarpone is a sinfully good cheese that, when fresh, is amazing just by itself, generously slathered on a piece of good bread. In specialty delis in Italy, such as Peck's in Milan or Tamburini in Bologna, it is displayed in decadent swirling mountains, like pristine white-capped peaks after a heavy snowfall. Fresh mascarpone barely lasts two or three days, but the packaged kind that is available in the States has a much longer shelf life and is fine when used in dishes such as this one and desserts. In this dish, where there is no cooking involved, prosciutto and mascarpone are simply mixed together and tossed with hot pasta, allowing their flavors to be the stars.

SERVES 4

4 ounces mascarpone (about ½ cup)

1 egg yolk

¼ cup freshly grated Parmigiano-Reggiano

Salt

4 ounces prosciutto, sliced ⅛ inch thick

1 pound spaghetti

1. Fill a pot for the pasta with about 6 quarts of water, place over high heat, and bring to a boil.
2. Put the mascarpone in the bowl you'll be serving the pasta in. Add the egg yolk, grated Parmigiano-Reggiano, and salt, and mix well. Cut the prosciutto into narrow strips about 1 inch long and mix it into the mascarpone.
3. When the water for the pasta is boiling, add about 2 tablespoons salt, add the spaghetti, and stir until all the strands are submerged. Cook until al dente.
4. When the pasta is about halfway done, put 2 tablespoons of the pasta water into the mascarpone mixture and mix it in well. When the pasta is done, drain it well, transfer to the serving bowl, toss vigorously with the sauce (I find it easiest to do this with a wooden spoon), and serve at once.

MACCHERONI *with* PANCETTA *and* RICOTTA

Maccheroni alla Pancetta e Ricotta

In this wonderfully simple and satisfying dish, the ricotta takes on the flavor of the pancetta and coats the pasta with a delicious creaminess. The parsley is mixed in at the end, its raw flavor adding freshness to the sauce.

SERVES 4

½ medium yellow onion

2 tablespoons butter

2 ounces pancetta, cut ⅛ inch thick

Salt

1 pound maccheroni (rigatoni is also good)

3–4 sprigs flat-leaf Italian parsley

1 cup whole-milk ricotta

Freshly ground black pepper

½ cup freshly grated Parmigiano-Reggiano

1. Fill a pot for the pasta with about 6 quarts of water, place over high heat, and bring to a boil.
2. Peel the onion and finely chop it. Put the butter in a 10-inch skillet and place over medium–high heat. As soon as the butter has melted, add the onion. Sauté until the onion turns a rich golden color, about 5 minutes.
3. While the onion is sautéing, cut the the pancetta into narrow strips about 1 inch long. When the onion is ready, add the pancetta and sauté until it is lightly browned but not crisp, 1 to 2 minutes, then set aside.
4. When the water for the pasta is boiling, add about 2 tablespoons salt, add the maccheroni, and stir well. Cook until al dente.
5. While the pasta is cooking, finely chop enough parsley to measure about 1 tablespoon. Put the ricotta in the bowl you'll be serving the pasta in. Season with salt and pepper, add the parsley and grated Parmigiano-Reggiano, and mix well.
6. When the pasta is done, drain well and transfer it to the serving bowl. Add the pancetta and onion, toss well until all the pasta is coated with the ricotta, and serve at once.

Fusilli *with* Pancetta, Peas, *and* Cream

Fusilli con la Pancetta e Piselli

Savory pancetta and sweet peas make a great combination. I don't use onion because I don't want to attenuate the rustic, forceful flavor of pancetta, which makes fusilli, with its ridges and firm texture, a perfect pasta choice.

SERVES 4

1. Fill a pot for the pasta with about 6 quarts of water, place over high heat, and bring to a boil.
2. Shell the peas, if using fresh.
3. Cut the pancetta into narrow strips about 1 inch long. Put the butter in a 10-inch skillet and place over medium-high heat. When the butter has melted, add the pancetta and sauté until it has lightly browned. Add the fresh or frozen peas and about ½ inch of water. Season with salt and pepper and cover the pan. Cook until the peas are tender, 6 to 8 minutes for frozen peas and about 15 for fresh.
4. When the peas are almost ready, add about 2 tablespoons salt to the boiling pasta water, add the fusilli, and stir well. Cook until al dente.
5. While the pasta is cooking, uncover the pan with the sauce, raise the heat, and cook until all the liquid has evaporated. Add the cream and continue cooking until it has reduced by about one-third, 2 to 3 minutes, then remove from the heat.
6. When the pasta is done, drain well, toss with the sauce and the grated Parmigiano-Reggiano, and serve at once.

1¾ pounds fresh peas (or 12 ounces frozen)

2 ounces pancetta, sliced ⅛ inch thick

3 tablespoons butter

Salt

Freshly ground black pepper

1 pound fusilli

¾ cup heavy cream

½ cup freshly grated Parmigiano-Reggiano

Farfalle *with* Peas *and* Lettuce

Farfalle ai Piselli e Lattuga

Although lettuce may sound like a strange ingredient for a pasta sauce, it adds sweetness and body to this one. A base of pancetta provides a savory counterpoint to its sweet flavor. The extra time needed to shell fresh peas is certainly worth the effort, but when they are not available, frozen peas will also work well.

SERVES 4

1. Fill a pot for the pasta with about 6 quarts of water, place over high heat, and bring to a boil.
2. Peel the onion and finely chop it. Put the butter in a 12-inch skillet, add the chopped onion, and place over medium heat. Sauté until the onion turns a rich golden color, about 5 minutes.
3. While the onion is sautéing, cut the pancetta into narrow strips about 1 inch long. Wash the lettuce leaves and coarsely shred them. Shell the peas, if using fresh.
4. When the onion is ready, add the pancetta and sauté until it loses its raw color, about 1 minute. Add the lettuce and the peas, if using fresh. Season with salt and pepper, add about ½ cup of water, cover the pan, and cook over medium heat until the peas are tender, about 15 minutes. If using frozen peas, cook the lettuce until it wilts completely, about 5 minutes, then add the peas, season with salt and pepper, add about ¼ cup of water, and cook, uncovered, over medium heat for 10 minutes.
5. While the sauce is cooking, finely chop the parsley to measure about 1 tablespoon. Add it to the sauce when it has about 5 minutes of cooking time left.
6. Once the parsley is in, add about 2 tablespoons salt to the boiling pasta water, add the farfalle, and stir well. Cook until al dente. When the pasta is done, drain well, toss with the sauce, and serve at once.

½ large yellow onion

3 tablespoons butter

2 ounces pancetta, sliced ⅛ inch thick

1 head Boston or Bibb lettuce

1¾ pounds fresh peas (or 12 ounces frozen)

Salt

Freshly ground black pepper

3–4 sprigs flat-leaf Italian parsley

1 pound farfalle

Fettuccine *with* Peas, Prosciutto, *and* Cream

Fettuccine ai Piselli e Prosciutto

This sauce is traditionally served in Emilia-Romagna with a combination of green and yellow egg noodles. The dish is called *Paglia e Fieno*, which means "straw and hay." If you can find good-quality dried green egg noodles, by all means serve this the way it was intended. Otherwise, the sauce is also perfectly wonderful with just yellow egg fettuccine. Though frozen peas work quite well, if you can get fresh peas I encourage you to use them.

SERVES 4

½ medium yellow onion

3 tablespoons butter

1½ pounds fresh peas
(or 10 ounces frozen)

4 ounces prosciutto, sliced
⅛ inch thick

Salt

Freshly ground black pepper

10 ounces dried egg fettuccine

¾ cup heavy cream

⅓ cup freshly grated
Parmigiano-Reggiano

1. Fill a pot for the pasta with about 6 quarts of water, place over high heat, and bring to a boil.
2. Peel and finely chop the onion. Put the butter in a 10-inch skillet, add the chopped onion, and place over medium-high heat. Sauté until the onion turns a rich golden color, about 5 minutes.
3. While the onion is sautéing, shell the peas, if using fresh. Cut the prosciutto into narrow strips, about 1 inch long. When the onion is ready, add the prosciutto and cook, stirring, until it loses its raw color, 1 to 2 minutes. Add the fresh or frozen peas and season with salt and pepper. If using fresh peas, add about ½ cup water. Cook until the peas are tender, 6 to 8 minutes for frozen and about 15 minutes for fresh.
4. Add about 2 tablespoons salt to the boiling pasta water, add the fettuccine, and stir until all the strands are submerged. Cook until al dente.
5. While the pasta is cooking, add the cream to the sauce. Cook over medium-high heat until it has thickened a little and reduced by about one-quarter, 1 to 2 minutes.
6. When the pasta is done, drain well, toss with the sauce and the Parmigiano-Reggiano, and serve at once.

Rigatoni *with* Onions, Pancetta, *and* Pecorino

※ *Rigatoni all'Amatriciana Bianca*

Also known as *Pasta alla Gricia*, this sauce is traditionally made with only guanciale (cured pork jowl, which is mellower than pancetta) and pecorino cheese, and no oil or onions. This is the "white" version of the famous Amatriciana sauce on page 146. It dates back to before tomatoes were introduced in Italy. Since guanciale is difficult to find in the States, I use pancetta. I add onions to give it a sweeter, mellower flavor and olive oil because pancetta has a lot less fat than guanciale. Though purists may shudder at my version, I think it is quite delicious.

SERVES 4

1. Fill a pot for the pasta with about 6 quarts of water, place over high heat, and bring to a boil.
2. Peel and finely chop the onion. Put the olive oil in a 10-inch skillet, add the chopped onion, and place over medium-high heat. Sauté, stirring often, until the onion begins to turn a rich golden color, 6 to 8 minutes.
3. While the onion is sautéing, cut the pancetta into narrow strips about 1 inch long. When the onion is ready, add the pancetta and season lightly with salt and generously with pepper. Cook until the pancetta is lightly browned, 2 to 3 minutes, then remove from the heat.
4. Once the pancetta is in the pan and the pasta water is boiling, add about 2 tablespoons salt to the boiling water, add the rigatoni, and stir well. Cook until al dente.
5. When the pasta is done, drain well, toss with the sauce and the grated pecorino, and serve at once.

1 small to medium yellow onion

4 tablespoons extra-virgin olive oil

2 ounces pancetta, sliced ⅛ inch thick

Salt

Freshly ground black pepper

1 pound rigatoni

3 tablespoons freshly grated Pecorino Romano

Penne *with* Asparagus *and* Prosciutto

Penne agli Asparagi e Prosciutto

This is one of our favorites in spring when sweet, meaty asparagus is in season. To infuse this sauce with a rich asparagus flavor, I save some of the water the asparagus cooks in and use it to deglaze the skillet.

SERVES 4

¾ pound asparagus

½ medium yellow onion

3 tablespoons butter

4 ounces prosciutto, sliced ⅛ inch thick

Salt

Freshly ground black pepper

⅔ cup heavy cream

⅓ cup freshly grated Parmigiano-Reggiano

1 pound penne (short fusilli or egg fettuccine are also good)

1. Fill a pot for the pasta with about 6 quarts of water, place over high heat, and bring to a boil.

2. Fill a 10-inch skillet (or asparagus cooker) with water, place over high heat, and bring to a boil.

3. Cut off the white, woody bottom part of the asparagus spears, then peel the remaining bottom third. Add 1 teaspoon salt to the boiling water, then gently slide in the asparagus. Cook until the asparagus is tender, 5 to 6 minutes, then lift it out and set aside. Save ½ cup of the water the asparagus cooked in.

4. While the asparagus is cooking, peel and finely chop the onion. Put the butter in a 12-inch skillet, add the chopped onion, and place over medium-high heat. Sauté until the onion has turned a rich golden color, about 5 minutes.

5. Cut the prosciutto slices into strips about ⅛ inch wide and 1 inch long. When the onion is ready, add the prosciutto and sauté until it loses its raw color, 1 to 2 minutes.

6. Cut the asparagus into 1-inch lengths and add them to the pan. Continue sautéing until the asparagus becomes lightly colored, 2 to 3 minutes. Add the saved asparagus water and continue cooking until the liquid has evaporated completely, loosening any browned bits on the bottom of the skillet.

7. Add about 2 tablespoons salt to the boiling pasta water, add the penne, and stir well. Cook until al dente.

8. While the pasta is cooking, add the cream to the asparagus and cook until the cream has thickened, 1 to 2 minutes. Remove the pan from the heat.

9. When the pasta is done, drain well, toss with the sauce and the freshly grated Parmigiano-Reggiano, and serve at once.

Spaghetti *with* Cauliflower *and* Pancetta

Spaghetti al Cavolfiore e Pancetta

Cauliflower is a relatively mild vegetable, so to use it successfully in a pasta sauce it's necessary to combine it with bold and savory flavors. This sauce works because of the generous amount of pancetta and because the cauliflower is sautéed long enough to concentrate its flavor. Also, the pasta is cooked in the same water the cauliflower is boiled in so it begins taking on the cauliflower flavor even before it's tossed with the sauce.

SERVES 4

1 medium clove garlic

4 ounces pancetta, sliced ⅛ inch thick

1 medium head cauliflower

⅛ teaspoon hot red pepper flakes

4 tablespoons extra-virgin olive oil

Salt

1 pound spaghetti

⅓ cup freshly grated Pecorino Romano

1. Fill a pot for the pasta with about 6 quarts of water, place over high heat, and bring to a boil.

2. Peel the garlic and finely chop it. Cut the pancetta into narrow strips about 1 inch long. Remove the leaves surrounding the cauliflower and cut off the stem.

3. When the water for the pasta is boiling, add the cauliflower and cook until tender, about 8 minutes. When the cauliflower is ready, lift it out of the pot and turn the heat down to a low simmer.

4. Cut the cauliflower into small ½-inch chunks and discard the core at the bottom.

5. Put the garlic, pancetta, hot red pepper flakes, and olive oil in a 12-inch skillet and place over medium-high heat. After the garlic begins to sizzle, add the cauliflower, season with salt, and sauté, stirring often, until the cauliflower is lightly browned, about 10 minutes.

6. After the cauliflower has sautéed for at least 5 minutes, raise the heat under the pasta water to high, add about 2 tablespoons salt, add the spaghetti, and stir until all the strands are submerged. Cook until al dente.

7. When the cauliflower is ready add about ¼ cup of the pasta water, loosen the browned bits from the bottom of the pan, and remove from the heat. When the pasta is done, drain well, toss with the sauce and the grated Pecorino Romano, and serve at once.

PAPPARDELLE *with* SHIITAKE MUSHROOMS

Pappardelle ai Funghi, Pancetta e Pomodorini

This is one of those instances where I use an ingredient that is more common in the States than in Italy in an Italian way. Whereas in Italy I would make this dish with fresh porcini, in the States I like making it with shiitake mushrooms. Though shiitake don't taste like porcini, their texture is similar, and I was particularly pleased with the way this sauce turned out using them.

SERVES 4

1. Fill a pot for the pasta with about 6 quarts of water, place over high heat, and bring to a boil.

2. Peel the onion and finely chop it. Put the butter in a 12-inch skillet, add the chopped onion, and place over medium-high heat. Sauté until the onion turns a rich golden color, about 5 minutes.

3. While the onion is sautéing, cut the pancetta into narrow strips about 1 inch long. Rinse the mushrooms and slice them approximately ¼ inch thick. When the onion is ready, add the pancetta and sauté until it loses its raw color, 1 to 2 minutes. Add the mushrooms, season with salt and pepper, and cook until tender, 6 to 8 minutes.

4. While the mushrooms are cooking, cut the tomatoes in half lengthwise. When the mushrooms are ready, add the tomatoes and season them lightly with salt. Cook until the tomatoes begin to break down, 4 to 5 minutes, then add the cream and continue cooking until the cream thickens, about 2 minutes. Remove from the heat.

5. After adding the cream, put about 2 tablespoons salt in the boiling pasta water, add the pappardelle, and stir until all the noodles are submerged. Cook until al dente.

6. When the pasta is done, drain well, toss with the sauce and the Parmigiano-Reggiano, and serve at once.

½ medium yellow onion

3 tablespoons butter

2 ounces pancetta, sliced ⅛ inch thick

6 ounces fresh shiitake mushrooms

Salt

Freshly ground black pepper

6 ounces grape tomatoes

½ cup heavy cream

10 ounces dried egg pappardelle

¼ cup freshly grated Parmigiano-Reggiano

FUSILLI *with* BUTTERNUT SQUASH

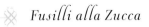

Fusilli alla Zucca

In Italy pumpkin would be used for this sauce, but I've found that butternut squash more closely resembles the flavor of Italian pumpkin than American pumpkin does. This sauce has been a hit with kids. I made this one day when my daughters had playmates over, and the five-to-nine-year-old crowd unanimously approved it!

SERVES 4

1. Fill a pot for the pasta with about 6 quarts of water, place over high heat, and bring to a boil.

2. Peel the onion and finely chop it. Put the butter in a 12-inch skillet, add the chopped onion, and place over medium-high heat. Sauté until the onion turns a rich golden color, about 5 minutes.

3. While the onion is sautéing, cut the pancetta into narrow strips about 1 inch long. Remove the ends of the butternut squash and peel it down to the orange flesh, taking care to remove all the green parts. Cut in half lengthwise and remove the seeds. Cut into $\frac{1}{2}$-inch dice. You should end up with approximately $1\frac{1}{2}$ pounds or 4 cups of diced squash.

4. When the onion is ready, add the pancetta and sauté until it is lightly browned, 1 to 2 minutes. Add the squash and season with salt and pepper. Stir well, then add 1 cup water and cover the pan. Cook until the squash is tender, 8 to 10 minutes.

5. When the squash is almost ready, add about 2 tablespoons salt to the boiling pasta water, add the fusilli, and stir well. Cook until al dente.

6. While the pasta is cooking, grate the pecorino cheese using the medium-sized holes of the grater. When the pasta is almost ready, mash the squash in the pan with a wooden spoon and mix in $\frac{1}{4}$ cup of the pasta water.

7. When the pasta is done, drain well, toss with the sauce and grated cheese, and serve at once.

½ medium yellow onion

3 tablespoons butter

2 ounces pancetta, sliced ⅛ inch thick

1¾ pounds butternut squash

Salt

Freshly ground black pepper

1 pound fusilli

3 ounces medium-aged pecorino cheese (such as Crosta Rossa di Pienza)

BUCATINI *with a* SPICY TOMATO SAUCE

Bucatini all'Amatriciana

This dish is named after the small town of Amatrice, about 100 miles northwest of Rome, though most people think of it as a classic Roman dish. In Rome it acquired onions and sometimes olive oil, and it is usually made with guanciale (cured pork jowl) rather than pancetta. In the following recipe I use onions, as in Rome; butter, because I like the creaminess it gives the dish; and pancetta, because guanciale is too difficult to find in the States. It's a sauce I will never tire of; just thinking of it makes my mouth water! The classic pairing is with bucatini, the thick, hollow spaghetti. Though not as authentic, it is also very good with penne or maccheroni.

SERVES 4

½ medium yellow onion

4 tablespoons butter

¼ teaspoon hot red pepper flakes

2 ounces pancetta, sliced ⅛ inch thick

2 pounds fresh tomatoes

Salt

1 pound bucatini (penne or maccheroni are also good)

½ cup freshly grated Parmigiano-Reggiano

2 tablespoons freshly grated Pecorino Romano

1. Fill a pot for the pasta with about 6 quarts of water, place over high heat, and bring to a boil.

2. Peel and finely chop the onion. Put 2 tablespoons of the butter and the hot red pepper flakes in a 12-inch skillet, add the chopped onions, and place over medium-high heat. Sauté until the onion turns a rich golden color, about 5 minutes.

3. While the onion is sautéing, cut the pancetta into narrow strips about 1 inch long. When the onion is done, add the pancetta and cook until it begins to brown, 1 to 2 minutes.

4. Peel the tomatoes and coarsely chop them. Add them to the pan and season with salt. Cook until the liquid they release has evaporated, 10 to 12 minutes.

5. When the tomatoes are about halfway done, add about 2 tablespoons salt to the boiling pasta water, add the bucatini, and stir until all the strands are submerged. Cook until al dente.

6. When the pasta is done, drain well and put it in a serving bowl with the two grated cheeses and the remaining 2 tablespoons butter. Stir vigorously until the sauce is creamy and thoroughly coats the pasta. Serve at once.

MACCHERONI *with* TOMATOES *and* SAGE

Maccheroni al Pomodoro e Salvia

This sauce is somewhat reminiscent of the flavors of a veal stew, even though the only meat present is a bouillon cube. A generous amount of butter and fewer tomatoes than in other tomato sauces give it a rich, sweet flavor. The sage is used whole and then discarded, scenting the sauce with its fragrance without dominating it.

SERVES 4

1½ pound fresh tomatoes

5 tablespoons butter

8–10 fresh sage leaves

Salt

Freshly ground black pepper

1 large bouillon cube

1 pound maccheroni (other tubular shapes are also good)

⅓ cup freshly grated Parmigiano-Reggiano

1. Fill a pot for the pasta with about 6 quarts of water, place over high heat, and bring to a boil.
2. Peel the tomatoes and coarsely chop them.
3. Put 3 tablespoons of the butter and the sage leaves in a 12-inch skillet. Place over medium-high heat. After the sage leaves begin to brown, add the tomatoes and season with salt and pepper. Add the bouillon cube, stirring until it dissolves, and cook until the liquid the tomatoes release has almost completely evaporated, 10 to 12 minutes.
4. When the tomatoes are halfway done, remove the sage leaves. Add about 2 tablespoons salt to the boiling pasta water, add the maccheroni, and stir well. Cook until al dente.
5. When the pasta is done, drain well, toss with the sauce and the grated Parmigiano-Reggiano, and serve at once.

PENNE *with a* SPICY TOMATO SAUCE

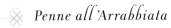
Penne all'Arrabbiata

Arrabbiata in Italian means "angry," because this is a spicy sauce. One does not often find spicy dishes in Italy, but in Rome and the surrounding area they are more common than in the rest of the country. The amount of hot red pepper here gives the sauce a medium heat. You can increase or decrease the amount, depending on how "angry" you'd like the sauce to be.

SERVES 4

1. Fill a pot for the pasta with about 6 quarts of water, place over high heat, and bring to a boil.
2. Peel the tomatoes and coarsely chop them. Peel and finely chop the garlic. Cut the pancetta into narrow strips about 1 inch long. Put 3 tablespoons of the olive oil, the garlic, the hot red pepper flakes, and the pancetta in a 12-inch skillet and place over medium-high heat. Sauté just long enough for the pancetta to lose its raw color and for the garlic to begin sizzling, 1 to 2 minutes, then add the tomatoes and season with salt. Cook for 5 minutes, then coarsely chop the basil and add it to the pan. Cook until the tomatoes have reduced and are no longer watery, 8 to 10 more minutes, then remove from the heat.
3. Add about 2 tablespoons salt to the boiling pasta water, add the penne, and stir well. Cook until al dente.
5. When the pasta is done, drain well, and toss with the sauce. Add the grated pecorino and the remaining tablespoon of olive oil, toss again, and serve at once.

1 medium clove garlic

2 ounces pancetta, sliced ⅛ inch thick

4 tablespoons extra-virgin olive oil

¼ teaspoon hot red pepper flakes

2 pounds fresh tomatoes

Salt

10–12 fresh basil leaves

1 pound penne

2 tablespoons freshly grated Pecorino Romano

Fusilli *with* Sausage *and* Zucchini

Fusilli alla Salsiccia e Zucchine

Savory sausage and sweet zucchini are a great combination, and adding some fresh tomatoes ties everything together. Try using a plain pork sausage instead of the Italian sausage, which in the States usually has fennel seeds, unlike most sausage in Italy. Or, since the casing needs to be removed anyway, make your own sausage mix using the recipe on page 161.

SERVES 4

½ medium yellow onion

3 tablespoons butter

8 ounces plain pork sausage (see note above)

12 ounces zucchini

Salt

1 pound fresh tomatoes

1 pound fusilli (shells are also good)

⅓ cup freshly grated Parmigiano-Reggiano

1. Fill a pot for the pasta with about 6 quarts of water, place over high heat, and bring to a boil.
2. Peel and finely chop the onion. Put the butter in a 12-inch skillet, add the chopped onion, and place over medium-high heat. Sauté until the onion just begins to turn a rich, golden color, about 5 minutes.
3. While the onion is sautéing, remove the casing from the sausage and break it up into pieces. When the onion is ready, add the sausage to the pan. Break the sausage up into small pieces with a wooden spoon and cook, stirring often, until the sausage is lightly browned, about 2 to 3 minutes.
4. While the sausage is cooking, wash the zucchini. Remove the ends, cut into quarters lengthwise, and then cut across into ½-inch chunks. When the sausage has lightly browned, add the zucchini. Season lightly with salt and cook until the zucchini begins to brown and is mostly tender, 6 to 8 minutes.
5. While the zucchini is cooking, peel the tomatoes and coarsely chop them. When the zucchini is ready, add the tomatoes, season lightly with salt, and cook until most of the liquid the tomatoes release has evaporated, 8 to 10 minutes.
6. When the tomatoes are halfway done, add about 2 tablespoons salt to the boiling pasta water, add the fusilli, and stir well. Cook until al dente.
7. When the pasta is done, drain well, toss with the sauce and the grated cheese, and serve at once.

Penne *with* Tomatoes *and* Prosciutto

Penne al Prosciutto e Pomodoro

In this tasty pasta dish, both prosciutto and pancetta are used. The pancetta is chopped and provides a rich, savory flavor base, while the prosciutto is cut into strips, adding texture as well as flavor.

SERVES 4

2 pounds fresh tomatoes

1 ounce pancetta, sliced thin

2 medium cloves garlic

3 tablespoons butter

2 sprigs fresh rosemary

Salt

Freshly ground black pepper

2 ounces prosciutto, sliced ⅛ inch thick

1 pound penne (maccheroni or other tubular shapes are also good)

1. Fill a pot for the pasta with about 6 quarts of water, place over high heat, and bring to a boil.
2. Peel the tomatoes and coarsely chop them. Chop the pancetta.
3. Peel and lightly crush the garlic cloves and put them with the butter and rosemary branches in a 12-inch skillet. Place over medium-high heat. When the garlic is lightly browned, remove it along with the rosemary, and discard. Add the pancetta and sauté until it loses its raw color, about 1 minute. Add the tomatoes and season with salt and pepper. Cut the prosciutto into narrow strips about 1 inch long and add them to the tomatoes. Cook until the liquid the tomatoes release has almost completely evaporated, 10 to 12 minutes.
4. When the tomatoes are halfway done, add about 2 tablespoons salt to the boiling pasta water, add the penne, and stir well. Cook until al dente.
5. When the pasta is done, drain well, toss with the sauce, and serve at once.

Farfalle *with* Salami *and* Tomatoes

Farfalle al Salame e Pomodoro

In Italy I would make this with a soppressa from the Veneto. It is thick, almost three inches in diameter, and quite soft. The best ones almost melt in your mouth. If you can't find something equivalent in the States, use any mild, soft salami.

SERVES 4

1. Fill a pot for the pasta with about 6 quarts of water, place over high heat, and bring to a boil.
2. Peel the onion and finely chop it. Put the butter in a 12-inch skillet, add the chopped onion, and place over medium-high heat. Sauté until the onion turns a rich golden color, about 5 minutes.
3. While the onion is sautéing, cut the salami into ⅛-inch dice. Peel the tomatoes and coarsely chop them.
4. When the onion is ready, add the tomatoes and the salami. Chop enough of the rosemary to measure about 1 teaspoon and add it to the pan. Season with salt and cook until most of the liquid the tomatoes release has evaporated, 10 to 12 minutes.
5. When the tomatoes are halfway done, add about 2 tablespoons salt to the boiling pasta water, add the farfalle, and stir well. Cook until al dente.
6. When the pasta is done, drain well, toss with the sauce, and serve at once.

½ large yellow onion

3 tablespoons butter

4 ounces soft, mild salami, sliced ⅛ inch thick

1½ pounds fresh tomatoes

1 branch fresh rosemary

Salt

1 pound farfalle (fusilli is also good)

PENNE *with* RADICCHIO

 Penne al Radicchio Rosso

Radicchio adds a refreshing, slightly bitter flavor to salads. When it is cooked, it loses some of its bitterness and makes a rich, luscious sauce. The Veneto region of Italy is known for the many varieties of radicchio grown there. The one from Treviso is the radicchio most often used in cooking. It is elongated and shaped a little like Romaine lettuce. The most prized is the one available in late fall called *tardivo*. It is distinguished by how the tops of its leaves curl in toward the center and by its rich, deep flavor. The most commonly available radicchio in the States is the round one from Chioggia, and it is perfectly fine in this recipe if the one from Treviso is not available.

SERVES 4

1. Fill a pot for the pasta with about 6 quarts of water, place over high heat, and bring to a boil.
2. Peel the onion and finely chop it. Put the butter in a 12-inch skillet, add the chopped onion, and place over medium-high heat. Sauté until the onion turns a rich golden color, about 5 minutes.
3. While the onion is sautéing, cut the pancetta into narrow strips about 1 inch long. Remove any bruised leaves from the radicchio, cut it in half lengthwise, and cut off the bottom of the root. Finely shred the radicchio.
4. When the onion is ready, add the pancetta and cook until it loses its raw color, 1 to 2 minutes. Add the radicchio and season with salt and pepper. Add about ½ cup water, lower the heat to medium, and cover the pan. Cook until the radicchio is very tender, about 20 minutes. Check it periodically and add more water if the liquid evaporates before the radicchio is tender.
5. While the radicchio is cooking, finely chop enough parsley to measure about 1 tablespoon.
6. After the radicchio has been cooking for at least 15 minutes, add about 2 tablespoons salt to the boiling pasta water, add the penne, and stir well. Cook until al dente.
7. When the radicchio is tender, uncover the pan, raise the heat, and let any remaining moisture evaporate. Add the cream and parsley and cook until the cream has thickened and reduced by about one-third.
8. When the pasta is done, drain well, toss with the sauce and the grated Parmigiano-Reggiano, and serve at once.

½ large sweet yellow onion

3 tablespoons butter

3 ounces pancetta, sliced ⅛ inch thick

1 pound radicchio

Salt

Freshly ground black pepper

3–4 sprigs flat-leaf Italian parsley

1 pound penne (fusilli is also good)

¾ cup heavy cream

½ cup grated freshly grated Parmigiano-Reggiano

TAGLIATELLE *with a* QUICK *and* SIMPLE MEAT SAUCE

Tagliatelle al Ragù Veloce

The classic Bolognese meat sauce gets its incredibly rich, succulent flavor from long, slow cooking. But what if you are in the mood for a meat sauce and don't have the three or four hours required? Here is a simple, quick version that you can make in about 30 minutes. I use fresh tomatoes rather than canned and no carrots, celery, wine, or milk. The result is a fresher, more direct, less complex flavor that sometimes fills the bill perfectly. My first choice of pasta for this sauce is egg noodles, but rigatoni or shells also make a good pairing. I recommend using beef chuck, which is about 20 percent fat, to keep the sauce moist. If you will be using a leaner cut, add a tablespoon of butter.

SERVES 4

½ medium yellow onion

2 tablespoons extra-virgin olive oil

1 tablespoon butter

1 pound fresh tomatoes

¾ pound ground beef chuck

Salt

10 ounces dried egg tagliatelle or pappardelle (or 1 pound rigatoni or shells)

⅓ cup freshly grated Parmigiano-Reggiano

1. Fill a pot for the pasta with about 6 quarts of water, place over high heat, and bring to a boil.
2. Peel the onion and finely chop it. Put the olive oil and butter in a 12-inch skillet, add the chopped onion, and place over medium-high heat. Sauté until the onion turns a rich golden color, about 5 minutes.
3. While the onion is sautéing, peel the tomatoes and coarsely chop them.
4. When the onion is ready, add the ground beef, season with salt, and cook, stirring, until it has lost its raw color and just begins to brown, 2 to 3 minutes. Add the tomatoes, season them with salt, and cook over medium heat until the liquid the tomatoes release has almost completely evaporated, 10 to 12 minutes.
5. Add about 2 tablespoons salt to the boiling pasta water, add the tagliatelle, and stir until all the strands are submerged. Cook until al dente.
6. When the pasta is done, drain well, toss with the sauce and the grated Parmigiano-Reggiano, and serve at once.

RIGATONI *with a* VEAL ROAST SAUCE

This sauce reminds me of the flavors of a classic pan-roasted veal rolled with pancetta and sage. I've added some tomatoes to make it into a sauce that will cling to the pasta, but otherwise the ingredients are pretty much the same, except that there is no wine. It's a sauce that would also go very well with ruote di carro (cartwheels) or shells, both of which have nooks and cavities to catch the meat.

SERVES 4

1. Fill a pot for the pasta with about 6 quarts of water, place over high heat, and bring to a boil.
2. Peel the garlic. Cut the pancetta into ⅛-inch dice. Peel the tomatoes and coarsely chop them.
3. Put the butter in a 12-inch skillet and place over medium heat. When the butter begins to melt, put the garlic cloves in. Let them brown lightly on all sides, then remove them.
4. While the garlic is browning, coarsely chop the sage. After removing the garlic, add the pancetta and sage. Sauté briefly until the pancetta loses its raw color, 1 to 2 minutes, then add the veal. Season with salt and cook, stirring often, until it begins to brown, 2 to 3 minutes. Add the tomatoes and season lightly with salt. Lower the heat to medium and continue cooking until most of the liquid the tomatoes release has evaporated, 10 to 12 minutes.
5. When the tomatoes are halfway done, add about 2 tablespoons salt to the boiling pasta water, add the rigatoni, and stir well. Cook until al dente.
6. When the pasta is done, drain well, toss with the sauce, and serve at once.

2 medium cloves garlic

1 ounce pancetta, sliced ⅛ inch thick

1 pound fresh tomatoes

4 tablespoons butter

10–12 fresh sage leaves

¾ pound ground veal

Salt

1 pound rigatoni (shells or cartwheels are also good)

BUCATINI *with* FRESH TOMATOES *and* THYME

Bucatini al Pomodoro e Timo

One of my favorite ways to serve beef tenderloin steaks is pan-seared with a quick sauce of fresh tomatoes, thyme, and a thin slice of pancetta on top. It's such a tasty sauce that I decided to make it into a pasta sauce, using chopped pancetta instead of whole slices.

SERVES 4

½ medium yellow onion

3 tablespoons extra-virgin olive oil

1½ ounces pancetta, sliced ⅛ inch thick

2 sprigs fresh thyme

2 pounds fresh tomatoes

Salt

1 pound bucatini

1. Fill a pot for the pasta with about 6 quarts of water, place over high heat, and bring to a boil.

2. Peel the onion and finely chop it. Put the olive oil in a 12-inch skillet, add the chopped onion, and place over medium-high heat. Sauté until the onion turns a rich golden color, about 5 minutes.

3. While the onion is sautéing, finely dice the pancetta. Finely chop enough thyme leaves to measure about 1 teaspoon. Peel the tomatoes and coarsely chop them.

4. When the onion is ready, add the pancetta and fresh thyme. Sauté briefly until the pancetta loses its raw color, about 1 minute, then add the tomatoes. Season with salt and cook until most of the liquid the tomatoes release has evaporated, 10 to 12 minutes.

5. When the tomatoes are halfway done, add about 2 tablespoons salt to the boiling pasta water, add the bucatini, and stir until all the strands are submerged. Cook until al dente.

6. When the pasta is done, drain well, toss with the sauce, and serve at once.

PENNE *with* MUSHROOMS *and* HAM

 Penne ai Funghi e Prosciutto

Dried porcini add richness of flavor to the white mushrooms here. An Italian prosciutto cotto is a ham that is slow-cooked with a minimum of herbs and spices and would be ideal here. If it is unavailable, use a good-quality plain cooked ham.

SERVES 4

1. Put the dried porcini in a bowl, cover with warm water, and soak for at least 10 minutes.

2. Fill a pot for the pasta with about 6 quarts of water, place over high heat, and bring to a boil.

3. Peel and finely chop the onion. Put the butter in a 12-inch skillet, add the chopped onion, and place over medium-high heat. Sauté until the onion turns a golden color, about 5 minutes.

4. Cut the ham slices into narrow strips about 1 inch long. When the onion is ready, add the ham and sauté until it browns, 2 to 3 minutes.

5. While the ham is sautéing, lift the porcini out of the water, squeezing the excess back into the bowl. Do not discard the water. Rinse the mushrooms under running water and chop them coarsely. When the ham is ready, add the porcini to the pan and season lightly with salt. Strain the porcini water through a paper towel and add to the pan. Raise the heat and cook until all the water has evaporated.

6. In the meantime, brush any dirt off the white mushrooms and cut into ¹/₂-inch dice. When all the porcini water has evaporated, add the diced mushrooms and season with salt and pepper. Lower the heat to medium-high and cook until all the water the mushrooms release has evaporated and they begin to brown lightly.

7. When the mushrooms are almost ready, add about 2 tablespoons salt to the boiling pasta water, add the penne, and stir well. Cook until al dente.

8. Add the cream to the pan with the mushrooms and cook until the cream has thickened and reduced by about one-third, 1 to 2 minutes. Remove the pan from the heat.

9. When the pasta is done, drain well, toss with the sauce and the freshly grated Parmigiano-Reggiano, and serve at once.

½ ounce dried porcini mushrooms

½ medium yellow onion

3 tablespoons butter

3 ounces prosciutto cotto or plain boiled or baked ham, sliced ⅛ inch thick

Salt

12 ounces white mushrooms

Freshly ground black pepper

1 pound penne

¾ cup heavy cream

⅓ cup freshly grated Parmigiano-Reggiano

SHELLS *with* SAUSAGE *and* CREAM

Conchiglie alla Salsiccia

This is the classic sauce that in Emilia-Romagna is served with gramigna, a short, curled egg pasta whose name means "crab grass" in Italian. The sausage that would be used in Italy is a plain, mild pork sausage. The mild or sweet Italian sausage available in the States always has fennel seeds, which unfortunately completely change the flavor of this dish. Try using a plain breakfast sausage instead or, since the casing needs to be removed anyway, make your own sausage mix using the recipe that follows.

SERVES 4

½ **medium yellow onion**

2 **tablespoons butter**

8 **ounces plain pork sausage (see note above)**

Salt

1 **pound conchiglie (fusilli is also good)**

¾ **cup heavy cream**

Freshly ground black pepper

½ **cup freshly grated Parmigiano-Reggiano**

1. Fill a pot for the pasta with about 6 quarts of water, place over high heat, and bring to a boil.

2. Peel and finely chop the onion. Put the butter in a 12-inch skillet, add the chopped onion, and place over medium-high heat. Sauté until the onion just begins to turn a rich, golden color, about 5 minutes.

3. While the onion is sautéing, remove the casing from the sausage and break it up into pieces. When the onion is ready, add the sausage to the pan. Reduce the heat to medium and break the sausage up into small pieces with a wooden spoon. Cook, stirring often, until the sausage is cooked through and is lightly browned, 10 to 12 minutes.

4. After the sausage has cooked for about 10 minutes, add about 2 tablespoons salt to the boiling pasta water, add the conchiglie, and stir well. Cook until al dente.

5. When the sausage is ready, add the cream and season lightly with salt and pepper. Cook until the cream has thickened and reduced by about one-third, 2 to 3 minutes, then remove from the heat.

6. When the pasta is done, drain well, toss with the sauce and the grated cheese, and serve at once.

HOMEMADE SAUSAGE

Sausage like that made in Italy is one of the hardest Italian products to find in the States. The sausage most often used in Italy is made with ground pork, salt, pepper, and maybe some wine and garlic. The recipe below is not real sausage, of course, because it has no casing, but for those times when crumbled sausage is called for, it works remarkably well.

MAKES 1 POUND

1. Peel and finely chop the garlic. Put all the ingredients in a bowl and mix thoroughly with your hands.

2. Wrap in plastic wrap and refrigerate overnight to allow the flavors to blend. Use within 2 days or freeze for up to 2 months. Defrost overnight before using.

1 small clove garlic

1 pound ground pork

1 teaspoon salt

1 teaspoon freshly ground black pepper

2 tablespoons dry white wine

FETTUCCINE *with a* SAVORY VEAL SAUCE

Fettuccine al Sugo di Vitello Saporito

Veal is quite mild and goes very well with green olives, which give it a little kick. I usually cook veal with butter, but olive oil is better suited to olives, so I make this sauce with olive oil but add a little butter at the end when I toss it with the pasta. Half a bouillon cube adds depth of flavor.

SERVES 4

½ medium yellow onion

2 tablespoons extra-virgin olive oil

1 pound fresh tomatoes

¾ pound ground veal

Salt

Freshly ground black pepper

¼ cup dry white wine

½ large beef bouillon cube

8 large Sicilian-style green olives

10 ounces dried egg fettuccine

1 tablespoon butter

1. Fill a pot for the pasta with about 6 quarts of water, place over high heat, and bring to a boil.

2. Peel the onion and finely chop it. Put the olive oil in a 12-inch skillet, add the chopped onion, and place it over medium heat. Sauté until the onion turns a rich golden color, about 5 minutes.

3. While the onion is sautéing, peel and coarsely chop the tomatoes.

4. When the onion is ready, add the ground veal, season with salt and pepper, and cook, stirring often, until the veal is lightly browned, 2 to 3 minutes. Add the white wine and let it bubble for about 1 minute to evaporate the alcohol. Add the tomatoes and bouillon cube, lower the heat to medium, and continue cooking until most of the liquid the tomatoes release has evaporated, 10 to 12 minutes.

5. While the tomatoes are cooking, slice the flesh of the olives away from the pits and coarsely chop it.

6. When the tomatoes are ready, add about 2 tablespoons salt to the boiling pasta water, add the fettuccine, and stir until all the strands are submerged. Cook until al dente.

7. Add the olives to the sauce and continue cooking over medium heat until the pasta is ready. When the pasta is done, drain well, toss with the sauce and the butter, and serve at once.

PENNE *with* SAUSAGE *and* RAPINI

Penne con la Salsiccia e Broccoletti

Bitter and salty foods often go very well together and here the slight bitterness of rapini (also known as broccoli rabe) complements the savoriness of pork sausage. Use either the homemade sausage on page 161 or a plain pork sausage with as few spices as possible.

SERVES 4

½ pound pork sausage
(see note above)

5–6 tablespoons extra-virgin olive oil

1 pound rapini (broccoli rabe)

Salt

1 pound penne

1 large clove garlic

Pinch of hot red pepper flakes

1. Fill a pot large enough to hold the rapini with water, cover, place over high heat, and bring to a boil.
2. Fill a pot for the pasta with about 6 quarts of water, place over high heat, and bring to a boil.
3. If using sausage links, remove the casing. Put the sausage in a 12-inch skillet with ½ cup water and place over medium-high heat. Break the sausage up into small pieces with a wooden spoon and cook until it has lost its raw color completely, 2 to 3 minutes, adding a little water if necessary. Once the sausage is ready, allow all the water to evaporate and sauté the sausage until it has browned lightly. If there is very little fat from the sausage, add 1 tablespoon olive oil. Transfer the sausage to a bowl using a slotted spoon.
4. While the sausage is cooking, trim the bottom of the rapini and wash in cold water. As soon as the water for the rapini is boiling, add 1 teaspoon salt and the rapini. Cook until tender, about 4 minutes after the water comes back to a boil. Drain and squeeze as much water out as possible by pressing the rapini in a colander with a spoon.
5. Add about 2 tablespoons salt to the boiling pasta water, add the penne, and stir well. Cook until al dente.
6. Peel and finely chop the garlic. Add the garlic and hot red pepper flakes to the skillet and sauté over medium heat for about 15 seconds, then add the cooked rapini. Sauté, stirring often, until the pasta is ready.
7. About 1 minute before the pasta is ready, add about ¼ cup of the pasta water to the rapini and loosen the cooking residue with a wooden spoon. Put the sausage back in the pan to heat it through.
8. When the pasta is done, drain well, toss with the sauce, and serve at once.

FUSILLI *with* SAUSAGE, RICOTTA, *and* FRESH TOMATOES

Fusilli alla Salsiccia e Ricotta

This tasty, creamy pasta sauce has no cream. Ricotta is stirred in at the end instead, giving a rich, luscious texture. I like it best with homemade sausage (see page 161), or you can use a mild sweet sausage, preferably without fennel seeds.

SERVES 4

1. Fill a pot for the pasta with about 6 quarts of water, place over high heat, and bring to a boil.
2. Peel and finely chop the onion. Put the butter in a 12-inch skillet, add the chopped onion, and place over medium-high heat. Sauté until the onion turns a rich golden color, about 5 minutes.
3. While the onion is sautéing, peel the tomatoes and coarsely chop them. If using store-bought sausage, remove it from the casing.
4. When the onions are ready, add the sausage and break it up into small pieces with a wooden spoon. Cook until it begins to brown, 2 to 3 minutes.
5. Add the tomatoes and season with salt and pepper. Lower the heat to medium. After 5 minutes, coarsely chop the basil leaves and add them to the sauce. Continue cooking until most of the liquid the tomatoes release has evaporated, about 5 more minutes.
6. Add about 2 tablespoons salt to the boiling pasta water, add the fusilli, and stir well. Cook until al dente.
7. When the pasta is almost ready, stir the ricotta into the sauce over medium heat for about 1 minute, then remove from the heat. When the pasta is done, drain well, toss with the sauce and the grated Parmigiano-Reggiano, and serve at once.

½ medium yellow onion

2 tablespoons butter

½ pound plain sausage (see headnote)

1 pound fresh tomatoes

Salt

Freshly ground black pepper

12 fresh basil leaves

1 pound fusilli

½ cup whole-milk ricotta

⅓ cup freshly grated Parmigiano-Reggiano

MEAT PASTAS • 165

ACKNOWLEDGMENTS

First and foremost, I'd like to thank my family. My wife, Lael, whom I adore, thank you for your unwavering love and support. My daughters, Gabriella and Michela, thank you for enduring so many pasta meals. It is a joy to cook for and with you. I will always be grateful to my parents for their inspiration. The taste memories of my childhood have shaped the way I cook.

My agent, David Black, thank you for your support, encouragement, and most importantly for your friendship.

Luisa Weiss, my editor, thank you for the enthusiasm with which you embraced this project.

I am grateful for the passion and vision of the team that helped create the beautiful images in this book. The photographer, Joseph De Leo, and his assistant, Kazuhito Sakuma; the food stylist, Toni Brogan, and her assistant, Sarah Abrams; and Kristi Blunt for all the props. It was an absolute pleasure working with all of you.

Finally, I'd like to thank all our friends who bravely tasted all the dishes I presented to them while working on this book!

CONVERSION CHARTS

WEIGHT EQUIVALENTS

The metric weights given in this chart are not exact equivalents but have been rounded up or down slightly to make measuring easier.

AVOIRDUPOIS	METRIC
¼ oz	7 g
½ oz	15 g
1 oz	30 g
2 oz	60 g
3 oz	90 g
4 oz	115 g
5 oz	150 g
6 oz	175 g
7 oz	200 g
8 oz (½ lb)	225 g
9 oz	250 g
10 oz	300 g
11 oz	325 g
12 oz	350 g
13 oz	375 g
14 oz	400 g
15 oz	425 g
16 oz (1 lb)	450 g
1½ lb	750 g
2 lb	900 g
2¼ lb	1 kg
3 lb	1.4 kg
4 lb	1.8 kg

VOLUME EQUIVALENTS

These are not exact equivalents for American cups and spoons but have been rounded up or down slightly to make measuring easier.

AMERICAN	METRIC	IMPERIAL
¼ tsp	1.2 ml	
½ tsp	2.5 ml	
1 tsp	5.0 ml	
½ Tbsp (1.5 tsp)	7.5 ml	
1 Tbsp (3 tsp)	15 ml	
¼ cup (4 Tbsp)	60 ml	2 fl oz
⅓ cup (5 Tbsp)	75 ml	2.5 fl oz
½ cup (8 Tbsp)	125 ml	4 fl oz
⅔ cup (10 Tbsp)	150 ml	5 fl oz
¾ cup (12 Tbsp)	175 ml	6 fl oz
1 cup (16 Tbsp)	250 ml	8 fl oz
1¼ cups	300 ml	10 fl oz (½ pint)
1½ cups	350 ml	12 fl oz
2 cups (1 pint)	500 ml	16 fl oz
2½ cups	625 ml	20 fl oz (1 pint)
1 quart	1 liter	32 fl oz

OVEN TEMPERATURE EQUIVALENTS

OVEN MARK	F	C	GAS
Very cool	250–275	130–140	½–1
Cool	300	150	2
Warm	325	170	3
Moderate	350	180	4
Moderately hot	375	190	5
	400	200	6
Hot	425	220	7
	450	230	8
Very hot	475	250	9

INDEX